D0069086

"This riveting book documents the jo renowned cardiologist and scientist in An adventurous read, the book makes the reader eager to find out the progress and outcome of treatment. Under the guidance of a monk, author Magda Heras navigated the book of Psalms for prayer and inspiration in each event she faced on her journey. Equipped with her strong faith and personal relationship with the Lord, Heras feared no evil, even as she walked through the darkest valleys of life. Her witness in connecting faith and science reminds us intellectuals to ponder the ever-important life questions, 'What good will it be for someone to gain the whole world, yet forfeit their soul? Or what can anyone give in exchange for their soul?'"

> —Dr. Kai-Nan An, PhD
> Professor Emeritus
> Mayo Clinic College of Medicine

"*Even Though I Walk* sets new criteria for spiritual direction: The Psalms are the revelatory text. This book breaks new ground for cancer treatment and care."

> —Mary Margaret Funk, OSB, author of *Renouncing Violence: Practice from the Monastic Tradition*

"*Even Though I Walk* captures the magnificent humanity and steadfast courage of Dr. Magda Heras. Through her spiritual pilgrimage with the increasing reality of a dwindling number of days in this life, Magda's writings inspire the most doubting skeptic. Knowing her in health was a joy and privilege but sharing her intimate ponderings as she approached death is a munificent treasure. This book should have special meaning to those who deny the intersection of faith and science or those who search in vain for a 'cat with five feet.'"

> —Michael B. Wood, MD
> Emeritus President and CEO, Mayo Clinic

"What a beautiful book this is—one about dying, yes, but at least equally about living well, with a fully human spirit open to deepening friendship, to the development of prayer life (especially through the medium of the Psalms), and to appreciation of the created world. Magda and Ignasi's correspondence is never saccharine or self-pitying; it acknowledges difficulties both spiritual and material. Yet it ultimately demonstrates—with instruction and reflection, questioning, lyricism, humor, and matter-of-fact description of the progress of cancer—how alive we can be, how much we can give each other even as life wanes. I wish I'd had this book when my husband was dying a decade and a half ago; I'm certainly going to share it with my hospice patients."

— Susan H. Swetnam, author of *In the Mystery's Shadow: Reflections on Caring for the Elderly and Dying*

"One of life's great challenges is to walk genuinely through the valley of the shadow of death with another human being, maintaining the mystery, not taking refuge behind easy, stock answers. This lovely book tells a story of when it happened— through unfailing relationships and through learning to pray the Psalms. Delicate, sensitive, and highly insightful."

— The Reverend Dr. James O. Chatham
Pastor, Presbyterian Church (USA)

"This book, while written in simple conversation, has a powerful message for all of us. Death comes in different ways but comes unavoidably to everyone. The dialogue between a Benedictine priest and an accomplished medical doctor reveals the tangle of emotions that emerge as the reality of death inexorably draws near. The book is not only enlightening but certainly worth a second reading."

— Irene Nowell, OSB, author of *Wisdom: The Good Life*

Even Though I Walk

One Woman's Journey of Prayer in the Shadow of Death

ACCOMPANIED BY A BENEDICTINE AND THE BOOK OF PSALMS

Magda Heras and Ignasi Fossas

Translated by Elaine M. Lilly

LITURGICAL PRESS

Collegeville, Minnesota

www.litpress.org

Cover design by Ann Blattner. Cover photos by Marc Garcia-Elias.

Originally published by Publicacions de l'Abadia de Montserrat as *Correspondència: Setembre 2012–Agost 2014; Descobrint la pregària dels salmistes* © 2016.

Scripture quotations taken from THE HOLY BIBLE, NEW INTER-NATIONAL VERSION,® NIV® Copyright © 1973, 1978, 1984, 2011 by Biblica, Inc.® Used by permission. All rights reserved worldwide.

Psalm 23 is from the ESV® Bible (The Holy Bible, English Standard Version®), copyright © 2001 by Crossway, a publishing ministry of Good News Publishers. Used by permission. All rights reserved.

© 2019 by Order of Saint Benedict, Collegeville, Minnesota. All rights reserved. No part of this book may be used or reproduced in any manner whatsoever, except brief quotations in reviews, without written permission of Liturgical Press, Saint John's Abbey, PO Box 7500, Collegeville, MN 56321-7500. Printed in the United States of America.

1   2   3   4   5   6   7   8   9

Library of Congress Cataloging-in-Publication Data has been requested.

ISBN 978-0-8146-8800-7   ISBN 978-0-8146-8825-0 (e-book)

Contents

Translator's Note

I am honored that Magda's family entrusted to me the translation from Catalan to English of this "spiritual documentary." Magda was a beloved friend and I heard her voice, in English, as I worked. I also heard the voice of her correspondent, Ignasi Fossas, in a brief but unhurried conversation in the monastery at Montserrat revered by many Catalans for spiritual, environmental, and/or cultural reasons.

I freely admit to a lack of "professional distance" in this translation. The process helped me to digest my grief at my friend's death, to celebrate having known her, and to keep a promise I made as she sought to confront her cancer diagnosis in some positive way: "Magda, maybe you're supposed to write something about this. If you do, I will help you." I'm a manuscript editor. That's what I do. But Magda didn't write a book. She wrote personal notes, as she always had—handwritten, emails, and "WhatsApp" text messages. Her communication with Fr. Ignasi was especially important to her as she faced mortality; their unique friendship became a great comfort to her—and now to me and others as well.

After her death, Magda's husband worked with Fr. Ignasi to compile excerpts of their correspondence, and bits of her periodic health updates for friends and family, for publication by the press at the Abbey of Montserrat. Fr. Ignasi added some context (shown in this font) and I've added a few explanations and brief notes [italicized, in square brackets]. A glossary, referenced by superscript numbers in the text, contains longer explanations and untranslated Catalan words, expressions, and cultural references. My favorite of these is a typical signature, *una abraçada* (a hug) or *petons* (kisses), which might puzzle the reader in translation. The welcoming embrace from Fr. Ignasi when we met and the parting benediction of a kiss on each cheek as I stood to leave are examples of how *abraçades* and *petons* show friendship and mutual respect. They are not translated in this book.

The best match for Bible translations tended to be the New International Version, except Psalm 23 (after the epilogue), which is from the English Standard Version. I have noted where I translated some portion of a verse quoted in Catalan or chose a different translation. The psalms are cited according to Masoretic numbering. All photos are from the family archives of Magda's husband, Marc Garcia-Elias. Sources for glossary entries are duly cited.

A personal note: I love the common Catalan expression of sympathy, "I accompany you in your sentiments" or more simply, "I accompany you." I use the short form, "*t'acompanyo*," and explain it to English-speakers like this: "It's almost one word, with just an apostrophe between us." Magda thanks Fr. Ignasi "for accompanying me in these difficult times," and I must thank both of them for accompanying me in this labor of love. I also thank those who graciously read drafts of the translation, including those who specifically helped this Lutheran kid attempt to do justice to the Catholic and Benedictine spirit of the correspondence.

Now, I leave you with the powerful prologue by Gabriel Magalhães, a Portuguese writer well known in Spain, and with the conversations, the pain, the spirit, the determination, and the tenderness of my friend Magda and the Benedictine who accompanied her toward her epilogue.

Elaine Lilly
Mankato, Minnesota, June 29, 2018

Prologue

Shining a Light in the Darkness

It is difficult to write these lines. Difficult because the book you now hold plunges into the mystery of pain and death. Faced with these somber, melancholic landscapes, our usual reaction is to look away. And say nothing. In fact, it is never easy to find words to say over cremation ashes or an open grave.

It is difficult, also, because in this volume we meet specific people, with names and surnames. On the one hand, there is Dr. Magda Heras, a distinguished Catalan cardiologist of international renown, who left a luminous professional and human legacy; on the other hand, Fr. Ignasi Fossas, also with a medical license but now a monk serving as the prior of the monastic community of Montserrat.

 During Dr. Magda's serious illness, she decided to engage in an intensive contact with Fr. Ignasi. One of the outcomes was what we could conventionally call a correspondence, although the forms of media used have almost nothing to do with the traditional paper and ink. Their dialogue floated in the sophisticated web of new technologies; we are confronted with an epistolary transfigured by contemporaneity.

And here we have that exchange, full of smiles, tears, and most of all questions. It is a whirlwind of emotions and thoughts, whose protagonists are Magda Heras and Ignasi Fossas, with secondary actors as well: Dr. Marc Garcia-Elias,

Magda's husband; other monks at Montserrat; and relatives and friends. And now the one writing these lines and you, reading these pages.

Do we have the right to listen to this chamber music of the approaching death, so very present in this dialogue between a monk and a woman who is ill? Yes, we do, and for a very simple reason: Dr. Magda Heras, who had generously offered her life to all who had the privilege of knowing her, decided to give us her death as well. In fact, from the beginning she shared her illness, intensely, with the people around her. And her death, the way she had to leave this world, reminds us a bit of the concept of a "last master class" of a great teacher.

There is, then, a lot to learn in these pages. First, this book is an adventure in prayer. We believers often transform our prayers into a long-suffering monotony. We pray as if walking home with a heavy bag of daily spiritual shopping. Sometimes without even realizing it, we impoverish what could be one of the secret treasures of a life story.

Driven by the river of life into the waterfall of death, Magda Heras, who had done so much scientific research, began a search for prayer with the same rigor she had applied in the laboratory. The result was that she discovered the immense ocean of biblical psalms, an ocean through which she sailed, discovering islands of consolation and sometimes verbal currents that allowed her to express her own internal tempests.

Her great discovery of the Psalms would be enough to make this book useful. How many of us pray using this spiritual heritage? Perhaps some of us, at most, hear psalms sung (sometimes off-key) at Sunday Mass, and our participation is reduced to echoing a refrain. Actually, the Psalms can live in us, as if creating a cathedral of the soul. The one who prays them finds in them the best mirror for the hard times in life, as well as for the bursts of existential joy.

Let us remember that Jesus himself, on the cross, prayed a psalm: "My God, my God, why have you forsaken me?"

(Ps 22:1). This phrase is not a recognition of defeat, as less-informed readers of the gospels might think, but rather a shout of hope in a moment of despair . . . because the one who asks the question still believes in an answer. And in that possible answer there exists, and persists, a presence: a light that, though surrounded by the shadows, is not extinguished. The Psalms, including the psalm that Jesus prayed, are a fortress of prayer that protects us so we can resist the onslaughts of life.

Magda's navigation through the Psalms would not have been possible without a human compass, which for her was Fr. Ignasi Fossas. The prior of Montserrat was like a map that does not prescribe any particular route. The task of this learned and loving priest consisted of explaining prayer's "wind rose" *[an ancient sailor's tool showing 32 directions and the eight winds]*, something he always did with exemplary humility, aware of what he did not know. Praying, of course, is also not knowing everything but yet not ceasing to recognize God in the swamp of doubts that sometimes show up in our prayers.

And that is how this trip toward the darkness was made in a ship of light: with Dr. Magda at the helm and Fr. Ignasi in the crow's nest, describing the horizon . . . because, indeed, the Abbey of Montserrat works a bit like the unfurled sails that allow navigation of the ship of Catalan spirituality. This book illustrates for us the relationship between the ethereal world of Montserrat and the more tangible cultural universe of Catalonia.

In fact, Dr. Magda went up to the "holy mountain," as many had done before her and many will do in the future. To "go up" (*pujar*—it must be said in Catalan to really ascend!) to Montserrat is an important part of Catalan identity. Many Catalans go up to this Benedictine abbey in order to truly be who they are, as if up there is a magic mirror that can allow us to see the transparency of our faces. For his part, Fr. Ignasi would also go down the mountain to visit his friend.

And the final result of these ascents and descents is a beautiful embrace of souls with no altitudes differentiating between them, only the purest Christian fraternity.

As a good scientist, Magda Heras appreciated innovation—which was reflected, for example, in her work as editor-in-chief of the *Revista Española de Cardiología,* the official journal of the Spanish Society of Cardiology. It is curious that the book you now hold in your hands also shows considerable novelty. In the Christian tradition, there are many volumes about pain. We have innumerable stories of martyrdom: severe fasting, hair shirts, and spiked belts appropriate for causing misery of the flesh; bare feet walking on sharp stones; and terminal illnesses narrated with beatific background music. There is even special language linked with these cases: the cross, atonement, reparation. This great dictionary of bitter suffering ends up transmitting the idea that pain is an accounting debt that must be paid to an implacable creditor (i.e., God).

Within this framework, some books are true horror stories because Christian spirituality, if misunderstood, gives rise to a terror film, staged with grim images from the darkest altars of the gloomiest churches. Not so with this book. What is surprising in Magda's correspondence is that, although there is pain, the suffering is expressed in today's words, using the most natural, everyday language. It is voiced without verbal affectation, without rhetorical sanctimony—in simple words, written by good people. It is a pain that speaks to us, seated by our side.

And this normality of language, this naturalness of word, is a great victory, an admirable merit of these pages. The merit is shared by Fr. Ignasi, who did not impose on his friend the verbal archaisms of faith—all those lexical dinosaurs that carry the believer away at times of suffering—and by Dr. Magda, who, in each message she sent, fought for honesty and transparency in the words she wrote. In this book, phrases flow with the naturalness of a coastline—clean and crystal clear; carrying sediments of pain, yes, but without the toxic spills of a dark religiosity.

Another curious aspect of this book is the articulation between faith and science. As we all know, we have been trying, over the last two centuries, to build a strange "Berlin Wall" between these two realities, as if believing implies ignorance and scientific knowledge automatically entails disbelief. One would therefore have to choose between the view through a microscope or telescope—which science has multiplied into an infinite number of new technological eyeballs—and the old religious vision, with its millennial myopias and astigmatisms. With its blindfolds, many atheists would say. Well, these pages prove it does not have to be like that. The eyes of Dr. Magda, trained by science, are open to the horizons of faith. And these two ways of seeing are complementary, not antithetical.

The dialogue between faith and science is particularly rich in this case because, on the one hand, we find a monk and a scientist together in the foreground of the stage. On the other hand, this dialogue also occurs *within* each of these characters: the friar studied medicine, in that past life that gets left behind in any radical profession of faith, and the scientist learns to become a nun in a convent without walls, shaped by her illness and her prayers.

And here I must confess that, although these pages abound in the merits I have mentioned, they leave an aftertaste of sadness. Gradually, we become covered with the dust of melancholy because all this work of prayer—by Magda Heras, by Fr. Ignasi, by the monks at Montserrat—hits a wall, the wall of death. And reading these pages we see how that wall approaches but we are unable to slow down the car that is our lives. An experience before which, as I said at the beginning, we would prefer to close our eyes.

In other words, in this book we hear that terrible silence of God we have all experienced at some time. I heard it so much that for a while it was very difficult for me to write this prologue. Faced with the life experience of Dr. Magda, who had transformed herself into an endless prayer without being able to avoid her death, everything in me was an Easter vigil that had not yet found the path to Alleluia Sunday. There are times when all we have of our faith is the desire to believe.

And that was how I remained mute and melancholic before the divine silence until, one day at the end of this past month of May, Dr. Marc Garcia-Elias came to visit me in the solitude of Covilhã, my own personal desert wilderness. The same divine silence that intimidated me was also pursuing him. We had a conversation that embraced the memory of his wife. He showed me a slide presentation about Magda, which was a beautiful declaration of love showing that the illustrious cardiologist had been a fragile and charming girl whose tenacity, bravery, and intelligence transformed her into a brilliant climber of all life's peaks. Not only the professional ones but also family ones, affective ones, endearingly human ones. And so her death also became a great climb—ideal for this woman who was passionate about the highest peaks of existence. As Dr. Marc and I talked, somehow God started speaking to us in the words that we exchanged. And when Marc Garcia-Elias left, stepping back onto that hectic carousel of doctors who are international icons, I had learned three important things.

First, there will always be, in our life of faith, a moment in which everything around us says "no" and we will have to say "yes." And at that moment our statement, in the midst of the darkness of such denial, will have a fundamental value. Magda Heras did it with her immense courage. And what we must hear, in the texts that she left us, is precisely the "yes" she wanted to say, and boldly said, without paying much attention to the "no" she also heard. We can hope that she will help us to be capable of a similar affirmation in the darkest hours of our own life stories.

Second, when we approach death, the essential thing is to reach that threshold with all of our humanity intact. Dying is only an insoluble problem if we are already dead when we die. Many deaths today are like the dying of the dead. To avoid this terrible death of the already deceased, euthanasia is now suggested: the maximum endpoint of a fearsome multiplication of mortalities. But, if we approach the river that separates us from the other life with everything we are, we will discover within ourselves the mysterious boat that will take us to the other shore.

This book is, in fact, a spectacle of humanity: the consummately human Fr. Ignasi and the radically human Dr. Magda. Death represents, in essence, a shipwreck that allows the best of our condition as men and women to survive. And that is what happens in these pages: an explosion of affection, tenderness, kindness. An existential embrace that can encompass everyone who wishes to be embraced. Because Christianity teaches us that our humanity, both the evil we commit or, as in this case, the good that we are capable of, is our common homeland.

And the third conclusion: we should not die in resignation, chewing on our demise as if it were a bitter medicine. We must extinguish ourselves by loving life, loving it deeply, because we are not abandoning it but moving toward the other side of it, toward the most intensely vivid dimension of the same life. This is one of the great lessons from Magda Heras: she did not die while nodding off in the shade, but while seeking the sunlight. Shortly before she died, she told her husband that she wanted to hike once more up the Tèsol, a beloved peak in the Pyrenees. This reaffirms the idea that to die is to finish our climb to life's summit, and not to just dive

into death's underwater grave. Our goal will not be to abandon the landscapes and the faces we love, but rather the
opposite: to put all of them, having developed them in the
darkroom of death, into our album for eternity.

In fact, Magda Heras did return to the Tèsol summit: Marc
Garcia-Elias placed a part of his wife's ashes on that moun-
taintop. It was as if he had buried his wife in the air. And we
must add that this book is also, in a sense, part of those ashes.
These texts are what remains of the luminous death of an
admirable woman who, in order to walk toward death, took
the hand of a learned and intelligent monk, who was at the
same time sensitive and pragmatic. The friar and the doctor
sing, in these contemporary messages, a psalm for two voices:
a spiritual duet that touches us, perhaps changing us as people.

A light shines on Son del Pi, a village at the base of El Tèsol

This book can also be defined as a dialogue between a living person who has died and a dead person who lives on. The living person who reminds us of a departed one is Fr. Ignasi, consecrated to a new life as a friar at Montserrat, a way of life in a mysterious no-man's land between this world and the one beyond. The dead woman who lives is Magda Heras. When we reach the end of this book, after we overcome the emotions of having read this very personal correspondence, Magda's absence infiltrates our lives as a friendly presence, a light shining in the darkness.

Meanwhile, the Abbey of Montserrat remains in the landscapes of Catalonia, Spain, and Europe. It stands like a portal to many mysteries, like the flight of prayers anchoring the fabric of our lives, like an ancient, profound Benedictine song that, every day, has new echoes. In short, it is a mirror reflecting the highest heights, in which each of us can find the truth in his or her face. Because we, like Dr. Magda, can go up to Montserrat and, doing that, one day reach, perhaps, the highest of all summits.

Gabriel Magalhães
Covilhã, Portugal, June 8, 2015

Introduction

I'd known Marc for years through the medical profession and through his involvement with our monastery. One Monday morning, September 24, 2012, to be exact, he called to see if I was at Montserrat. He wanted to come up with his wife, Magda, to visit me. We met in the community's reception area after Conventual Mass.[1] After the usual greetings, Magda excused herself to go to the washroom and Marc updated me about his activities, but quickly told me that this was not the reason for the visit; there was other news. Magda returned and told me about the diagnosis[2] she had received just a few days earlier.

All three of us are doctors and know how to keep an emotional distance when we discuss patients, but in this case the patient was there, in front of me, and I was impressed with her serenity. I became increasingly "touched," and I had no idea what to say. But my emotions reached their fullest when Magda finally said, "As you can imagine, everyone suggests things to do and special techniques to cope with the situation. To be honest, at this point only two things interest me: my oncologist's advice and if you can teach me to pray."

I couldn't move. Magda and I didn't know each other well, but I knew she was asking me for the only genuine thing that I could offer her at that point. It seemed that Providence had prepared everything. And so of course I humbly agreed to accept both this gift and the responsibility that was being offered to me.

Thus began a last-minute friendship (as in the parable of the Workers in the Vineyard: I arrived at the end of the day and received the same as those who were there from the first hour!), a fabric woven of personal conversations, emails, WhatsApps, and so many other little things that make up everyday life. And with that friendship came access to a reality to which I have been, through grace and the goodness of Marc and Magda, an exceptional witness—and for that I can never be sufficiently grateful.

The following texts are a selection of emails and messages that Magda and I exchanged. I have added some notes to help the reader better understand the text. I have also inserted fragments of letters that Magda regularly sent to friends and relatives, explaining the evolution of her illness. It goes without saying that, together with Marc, I undertook this task with great emotion and with great respect and veneration. I hope this book can help those who read it as much as my friendship with Magda has helped me.

Ignasi M.
Montserrat, September 24, 2014

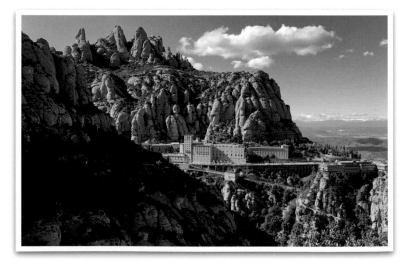

The Benedictine Monastery at Montserrat

Correspondence

September 12, 2012

Dear family and friends:

Yesterday I found out that the cough and shortness of breath that I've been having in recent months are caused by a lung tumor. . . . Gosh-darn-it-all,[3] what news! Frankly, I really wasn't happy about setting aside what I was doing to focus on getting well, but there is no alternative and I plan to do everything necessary so that years from now we can talk about it in the past tense.

I am not the first in the family and probably not the last to have a tumor. I'm sure those who have been through it will help me with the practical aspects of facing it day-to-day, and I plan to be a diligent student. In addition, I hope that all of you will have some time to spend with me (going for a walk or for coffee, suggesting pastimes, good books, music, etc.).

I intend to continue living life as normally as possible and not stay home gazing at my navel, so I will go to concerts and the theatre and hope to be able to see more cinema than usual. Today I will have a more extensive visit with the pneumologist, tomorrow a PET scan (that's Positron Emission Tomography), and Thursday a bronchoscopy (with anesthesia!). When I have more details, I will share them.

We don't want to have any secrets from our friends and family, including our parents and our daughter. Marc and I believe that if everything is out in the open everyone will be better able to help me. Tell the youngest children that I'll explain it to them when we get together to celebrate September birthdays. Next June I'll be 60 and the celebration will be a special one.

Petons,[4] Magda

September 14, 2012

Dear friends and family:

Today they did the PET scan. It was important to determine whether any other part of the body showed evidence of an additional tumor. Eureka! I only have one, on the right lung, the same one that showed on the computed axial tomography (CAT) scan—so today's scoreboard stands at 1-0! Some of you might think this delight is exaggerated, but for me it was very important to have this information and I'm happy with it.

The next round is a bronchoscopy on Tuesday. They'll take samples for pathology analysis, and next Thursday we'll know the type of tumor, and Friday they'll decide on treatment.

I am very happy with the way I'm treated at Hospital Clínic. Everybody is waiting for me when I arrive and they're familiarized with my case. Both the anesthesiologist and pathologist have called me to talk about things. I really couldn't ask for anything more. And what's more, everybody shows affection for me . . . what a luxury!

Magda

Magda / September 25, 2012

Dear Ignasi:

I know you are very busy and that somebody giving you a little more work is probably not what you really want. Nonetheless, I very much appreciated our conversation because it was an opportunity to talk with a medical colleague who understands disease but also has a spiritual dimension that I lack.

I haven't talked with you very often; in fact, the last time I saw you was when you were the financial administrator *[for the monastic community at Montserrat]*. I guess you and Marc have seen each other more often, for professional reasons. In any case, and to be brief, I would just tell you that both of us are highly dedicated to the medical profession: I teach at the University of Barcelona—residents, students—and direct doctoral dissertations, attend national and international conferences, do basic and clinical research, get grants, participate in working groups of national and international societies, etc. Marc has also done all that, and in our life together, which is and has been very pleasant, we have been 100% dedicated to our work. We have a 31-year-old daughter, Anna, a biologist who works in cell electrophysiology and now has her doctorate and teaches at Pompeu Fabra University.

We really enjoy nature, and our ideal getaway is walking in the mountains, or skiing, snowshoeing, etc. In fact, this summer we spent four sensational weeks in the Pallars Sobirà,[5] where we have designed a house that we love. I hope that someday you will come to Isil to see it.

As I guess you can easily imagine, a diagnosis like this changes life in an instant. What was essential and urgent becomes totally secondary, and many things that had been put off or were "hibernating" (that's something we cardiologists say, "hibernating myocardium," meaning the myocytes are alive but not pulsating due to inadequate blood flow) begin to surface with increasing intensity and persistence.

Isil, Pallars Subirà

This whole introduction is my way of telling you that I'd like to spend some time every day in spiritual reflection and prayer. I am not sure how to start and that's why I'm asking for your help. Obviously, I don't want some kind of "How to pray in one hour" short course, just some guidance on getting started, texts that could help me, etc.

I grew up in a Catholic family, but with two interesting approaches: my father believes that one must fulfill the obligations (Masses, communions, baptisms, etc.); my mother, who goes to Mass almost every day, has a faith that is more like mine. She says that we don't have to spend all day crossing ourselves, but we should maintain a dialog with One who loves us, and explain and ask for help with the things that worry us, feeling that God is near even if "it's been a few years" since we've maybe even said hello.

Anyway, while I am waiting for the pathologist to tell me about my tumor, I've taken the opportunity to write you. If you have a little time and want to spend it on me, I will appreciate it very much. I'm on sick leave, so I could come to Montserrat again someday, even though modern technology allows for more "virtual" contact. My brother comes up to the *Escolania*[6] and I could ride along with him.

Just as I have taken the liberty of asking you this, I hope you will do the same and freely tell me whether you have a little time to spend with me.

Of all the possible "esoteric" or "natural" or "alternative" therapies everyone is recommending, and it seems that many people believe in them, I am only interested in the ones my oncologist and you can offer me.

Thank you for the opportunity to be in contact with you.

Ignasi / September 27, 2012

Your email made a big impression on me. In fact, I was also strongly impressed during your visit, of course. You are asking me for one of the most beautiful things a monk can share with others: prayer and the cultivation of a spiritual life. But at the same time, it is one of the most difficult things, because it is a very delicate subject that surpasses our understanding and in which I feel like an apprentice—like an R1 *[first-year resident, a physician undergoing supervised training in a specialty]*, so you know what I mean.

I therefore agree to your proposal with enthusiasm, and also accept with fear and trembling (with fear and with a chill = with much respect) because you invite me to accompany you on a path that travels through the human heart—that is to say, through a sacred terrain. I will try to open my heart as a brother and share with you what I have learned about prayer.

Without further preamble, let's get to the point.

The Christian prayer par excellence is the "Our Father," the Lord's Prayer. Ah, but first I wanted to tell you that in the Rule of Saint Benedict,[7] when he speaks of the attitude of monks toward the oratory *[a monastic space for community and personal prayer]*, he says that our minds (our spirits, our hearts) must be "in harmony with our voices" *[RB 19.7].* The monastic tradition teaches that the vocal repetition of certain prayers helps us to pray, as if tenderizing the heart, lovingly, and along the way it helps to focus and guide our thought and imagination toward the things of God.

I return to the Lord's Prayer. I said that it is the Christian prayer *par excellence.* It is what Jesus taught his disciples when they asked that he teach them to pray. Sometimes it happens that these very well-known texts become almost irrelevant to us. It helps me to read them in other languages, because it seems to me that I hear them for the first time and there is always some new word or some new expression. The early Christians had the habit of praying the Lord's Prayer three times a day: in the morning, at noon, and in the evening. It's a good way to start.

There is a book that I like very much, although when it was published it received some criticism: the *Catechism of the Catholic Church.*[8] It is divided into four parts, and the last one is devoted to prayer. You will find a beautiful commentary on the Lord's Prayer. In addition, the whole fourth part is a very good introduction to prayer, without forgetting an important aspect: the struggle of praying. It is not easy to pray, and this must be kept in mind so that you do not get discouraged when you think you don't know how, or think that you are not making progress in prayer.

In addition to the Lord's Prayer, the Bible offers us an entire book of prayers, the book that Jesus used to pray: it is the book of Psalms. But we can talk about that another day.

I send *una abraçada*[4] and greetings to Marc.

September 29, 2012

Dear friends:

I just found out that I got the best lung tumor in existence. It's a tumor that has a mutation on exon 19 of the epidermal growth factor receptor . . . no need to make a face of disgust nor of ignorance (like mine until about 10 minutes ago). The good news is that there is a specific chemotherapy that attacks the cells with this mutation by using a monoclonal antibody that is very effective! Besides, it's an oral chemotherapy, one pill/day. The secondary effects are that I might get pimples on my face, discolorations on my skin, and I'll have to be well hydrated with lotions and use gentle soaps (like those for little kids).

My oncologist told me this with a relieved look on her face (it's not easy to give bad news, and even harder when it's a colleague) and I had to hold onto my chair to keep from throwing my arms around her neck! The alternatives were not very optimistic.

In fact, today I took the first pill. For now, I'll be on leave for three months and will have monthly check-ups. I don't need to tell you how much relief I feel and I'm sure you all share it with me (better said: with us, because Marc, Anna and Xavi have been worrying too).

I want to thank you for accompanying me these days, in person, at a distance, and in some cases "virtually"; you've helped me so much to get through these 16 days that have seemed so very long.

I am also very happy to have lived through all of this quite serenely and calmly, and we have had times of fun and normality that have been vital for me. Now Marc and I are going to Isil for several days to rest, but I will be able to get all the email, WhatsApps, and phone calls you want to send!

I love you lots,
Magda

Magda / October 10, 2012

I attach an "update" on my health. Many thanks for your support.

October 10, 2012

Dear ones:

Today was the first appointment with my oncologist after 12 days of the treatment that has totally brought my symptoms under control. It also has side effects that are visible on my skin (but very tolerable).

She said this was good news. Next appointment is in two weeks, with lab tests, and if everything is going well, monthly follow-ups. This will be long-term, but I feel so much better that I'm no longer in a hurry! In addition, I can do any exercise I want, even swimming!

I am very grateful for this oral chemotherapy (1 pill/day) that targets the type of tumor I have. What impresses me the most is that it has only been in use for two years!

I think I've been very lucky. . .

Un petó,[4] Magda

Ignasi / October 10, 2012

What joy, Magda! There is a Psalm that says: "In peace I will lie down and sleep, for you alone, O Lord, will keep me safe" (Ps 4:8).

Magda / October 19, 2012

I followed your advice: I prayed the Lord's Prayer, bought the books, and am reading the section about the Lord's Prayer that you recommended. I have the book of Psalms but haven't opened it yet.

If you have a little time some Tuesday, I'd like to come up and talk about it. I say Tuesday because I could ride with my brother, but it could be any day and time. I'm on sick leave and have time available, a luxury considering my "previous life." I'm also not in any hurry and it doesn't have to be immediately, simply when you can and when you feel like it.

The big news today is that I swam for half an hour without gasping for breath, for the first time since the diagnosis; as you can imagine, I am very happy. Wednesday I go in for tests (to rule out any kidney problems from the drug therapy) and see the oncologist.

I'm very grateful you're willing to help me.

October 25, 2012

Dear ones:

Yesterday I had the first lab tests and oncology visit after four weeks of treatment. The results were normal and my clinical progression very good. The side effects continue to be tolerable, especially considering the alternative . . .

We'll continue this treatment four more weeks, with the next lab tests on November 22nd and a new CAT scan before Christmas.

I can keep doing "life as normal" and all the exercise I want.

Since Marc was going off to Madrid, I went along, and I felt really good, in good shape and without limitations. You can imagine how happy I was about that, and I wanted to share it with all of you who are staying so closely by my side.

Magda

Tuesday, October 30th, Magda and I met at Montserrat. She came with her brother Lluís, who teaches music classes at the Escolania. This began a series of personal meetings that occurred in parallel to our correspondence. Therefore, the reader of this text must understand that it is only part of our dialogue; there is another part that took place, at a more or less regular cadence, and also forms part of the surprising and beautiful fabric of my relationship with Magda.

Magda / November 7, 2012

I started with the Psalms as you recommended . . . and it's not easy, as you also said. For now, I've gotten to 9 or 10 because I've reread many of them morning and evening. I think I prefer to reread them in order to understand them better. It seems strange to me that they are prayers while at the same time it's more like an intellectual challenge to analyze them from a literary perspective: to whom the psalmist is speaking, the different levels of conversation, changing situations, unusual use of language, "antiquated" situations, etc.

You can see that I need a lot of practice, but I wanted to comment on this "first week with the Psalms." I suppose that what I'm telling you is pretty normal . . . any guidance from you will be most welcome.

On Monday I went with some friends to receive a grant awarded to us from the TV3 Marathon.[9] It was a great joy (which is important to me these days) because it will allow us to continue our research on a pig model of heart attack for three more years. During the award ceremony, they showed a video with highlights of the marathon itself, and one of the clips was the *Escolania* singing with Sergio Dalma. I was thinking then that I should tell you about it.

Physically, I continue to do very well; right now I'm spending two days in Lausanne with Marc, who is operating on a patient. This city is sensational, on the shores of Lake Geneva and with the Alps on the other side, snow-covered already! The sunset was spectacular . . . I'll look for a Psalm that's appropriate.

Thank you for your time and patience.

Sailboat on Lake Geneva (Lausanne, Switzerland)

Ignasi / November 7, 2012

Thank you, Magda, for sharing your first impressions.

Tomorrow I will try to write when I have more time.

For now, as you observe "the spectacle" of Lake Geneva, try reading Psalm 19: the wonders of God in Creation and in the human heart.

Greetings to Marc.
Una abraçada

Psalm 19

¹ The heavens declare the glory of God;
    the skies proclaim the work of his hands.
² Day after day they pour forth speech;
    night after night they reveal knowledge.
³ They have no speech, they use no words;
    no sound is heard from them.
⁴ Yet their voice goes out into all the earth,
    their words to the ends of the world.
In the heavens God has pitched a tent for the sun.
    ⁵ It is like a bridegroom coming out of his chamber,
    like a champion rejoicing to run his course.
⁶ It rises at one end of the heavens
    and makes its circuit to the other;
    nothing is deprived of its warmth.
⁷ The law of the LORD is perfect,
    refreshing the soul.
The statutes of the LORD are trustworthy,
    making wise the simple.
⁸ The precepts of the LORD are right,
    giving joy to the heart.
The commands of the LORD are radiant,
    giving light to the eyes.

⁹ The fear of the LORD is pure,
  enduring forever.
The decrees of the LORD are firm,
  and all of them are righteous.
¹⁰ They are more precious than gold,
  than much pure gold;
they are sweeter than honey,
  than honey from the honeycomb.
¹¹ By them your servant is warned;
  in keeping them there is great reward.
¹² But who can discern their own errors?
  Forgive my hidden faults.
¹³ Keep your servant also from willful sins;
  may they not rule over me.
Then I will be blameless,
  innocent of great transgression.
¹⁴ May these words of my mouth and this meditation of
  my heart
  be pleasing in your sight,
  LORD, my Rock and my Redeemer.

Ignasi / November 22, 2012

On November 7th, I wrote in an email that "tomorrow I will try to write when I have more time" and I have not done it until today, the 22nd. I can't believe the days go by so quickly.

I will go straight to the subject of the Psalms. A characteristic of these poems is that they reflect all the situations a human person can go through. This has the advantage of allowing us to find words for each situation, both personal and collective. I've spent a little time copying down a few examples.

The Psalms reflect the entire (spiritual) experience of the human being:

Situation	Psalm Number
• When you want to praise the Lord	135
• When you want to know how and why you should praise Him	146
• When you feel joy and wonder before God for creation	8
• When you feel joy and wonder in the human heart for creation, looking at the sky and seeing [God's] Law	19
• When you want to make someone happy	128
• When your own persecute you	3
• When it seems arrogance and evil are multiplied; there are no good people anymore	12
• When the pain becomes unbearable and you say: "How long, O Lord?"	13
• When you feel weak and defeated by the anguish of life	102
• When you repent after having sinned	51
• When you feel a desire for God	42–43
• When you feel accused by an evil king	52
• When you want to sing a hymn to the Lord	65
• When you feel surrounded by enemies	109
• When enemies surround you and you want to lift up a prayer to God	25:1, 9
• When you feel envious of the unjust	73
• On Sunday	24 & 118
• On Monday	48
• On Wednesday	94
• On Friday (psalm recited by Jesus on the cross on Good Friday)	22
• On Saturday	92
• To celebrate the victory of the cross	93
• When you feel grateful to God, who accompanies you and guides you along the path of life	23
• When you want to express trust in God	125 & 130
• In the morning	5 & 63
• At night	141
• Before going to sleep	4 & 9
• To sing of faithfulness to God while in exile	137
• To praise God	148, 149, 150

The list is not exhaustive; it's just a sample.

This requires an effort, on our part, to familiarize ourselves with this language; at first, it demands that we leave our own selves behind and enter a world that can seem very different to us. But, little by little, we realize that these are words that become "ours."[10]

I think it is very important to be able to find words or expressions for different situations in life. Basically, it is about finding a way to express not only our feelings, but also the meaning of what we are living through.

Progressively, too, the Psalms reveal the face of the people of Israel, the face of the Messiah, the face of Christ. But that is another step.

I leave it here for today. Forgive the delay.

November 23, 2012

Dear ones:

I just had my second set of lab tests and an oncology visit after 56 days of treatment. Perfect lab results, and I had a very good clinical review; no symptoms. I'm physically active and working from home on things for the journal and other projects I can do online.

The conversation with the oncologist clarified things. She proposes long-term treatment with the current drug, for at least two years, and a scan of the lungs every three months. The first one will be December 21st, so there will be news by Christmas.

Definitely good news that must be celebrated. I'm certain that you will also be happy to hear about it.

Magda

Magda / November 26, 2012

Thanks for our visit yesterday. It's really good for me to maintain contact with you because it helps me a lot in "delicate" moments, which I do have, but fortunately they are few.

This morning I found the psalm I needed when I woke up: Psalm 28! I'm sure I will repeat it when I feel a little "down." I don't know, though, if this insistence on always asking for help is "correct" or if one should rather have the confidence that what you need is already known and you don't have to insist.

Maybe these doubts seem mundane to you, but I often ask myself these questions.

Ignasi / November 27, 2012

As I told you that first day, contact with you and Marc is also good for me.

I'm glad you are already finding psalms for each moment and for each situation. I do not believe that there's any problem with always asking the Lord to help us. Obviously, he already knows what we need, but it is good for us to explain it, to verbalize it (this is an anthropological need, because it is when things, impressions, feelings, convictions "pass" through our senses that we really make them our own[10]).

In addition, very often in the psalms that ask for help there is a point at which praise to God appears (this is the case with Psalm 28 itself, which says: "Praise be to the Lord, for he has heard my cry for mercy"). It is as if the psalmist, carried away by trust in the Lord, already sees the salvation he was asking for.

Next Sunday we will begin the Advent season. There are two characteristic psalms for this time, 25 and 80.

Magda / December 7, 2012

On Wednesday I had a follow-up CAT scan. There was a clear improvement after ten weeks of treatment. It's a magnificent bit of news that I wanted to share with you and for which I am very thankful.

We are in Isil[5] and today we went skiing; what an incredible feeling of freedom and normality. This was one of the activities I had "given up" in September. I'm sending you a photo of the snow-covered pines we saw while skiing. Even though you're more "urban," I'm sure you will appreciate the beauty of the photo. There was no sun, but for me today was radiant!

Bonaigua Pass, as seen from Baqueira, Val d'Aran

Ignasi / December 7, 2012

Oh, what joy! And what beauty!

This morning, at Lauds, we chanted Psalm 100. And at Vespers we will chant Psalm 113. Good psalms to sing on a radiant day.

Magda / December 8, 2012

Very appropriate ones for yesterday. I prayed them in the evening. It's still snowing. . .

Psalm 100

> Shout for joy to the LORD, all the earth.
> 2   Worship the LORD with gladness;
>   come before him with joyful songs.
> 3 Know that the LORD is God.
>   It is he who made us, and we are his;
>   we are his people, the sheep of his pasture.
> 4 Enter his gates with thanksgiving
>   and his courts with praise;
>   give Thanks to him and praise his name.
> 5 For the LORD is good and his love endures forever;
>   his faithfulness continues through all generations.

December 22, 2012

Dear ones:

As I told you in my last message, yesterday was the three-month review of my treatment. The CAT scan (radiology) showed a clear improvement, with a reduction in the lymphangitis, the tumor, and the middle lobe re-expansion. The lab tests were good too, so I can stay on this treatment another month.

I'm still living life as normal, but am on sick leave even though I still work on some research projects I have with hospital colleagues. I can do everything on my own time schedule, and it's really good for me to keep in touch and fill my time with things that interest me. I have also improved physically and am very active, with very few limitations. All I can say is that I am very happy. At the time of the diagnosis it wasn't at all clear that I would be able to celebrate Christmas as I will now, and for that I am very grateful.

Magda

Magda / January 15, 2013

Tomorrow I have another onco appointment and if everything is OK we will leave next week for a vacation in Austria. When I get back, could we look for another time to talk more about prayer? I'm on Psalm 109 and some of the recent ones are long and "hard," but I persist. . .

January 16, 2013

Excerpts from Magda's reply to an email from Marc's Aunt Griselda, a Benedictine nun at the Barcelona monastery Sant Pere de les Puelles:

Thank you, Griselda, for your email.

. . . about reading the Old Testament, I understand very well that you need to know what the original said, in Greek or Hebrew. In fact, I talk quite often with Ignasi Fossas at Montserrat, who has been guiding me on the topic of prayer, and he, too, always talks about the origins and the basic languages (Hebrew, Greek, and German). I have to acknowledge that, thanks to him, I'm "dusting off" my prayer life, which was pretty neglected, although I am always aware that God is near and loves me. Ignasi helps me with this, and I believe it has also given me a lot of peace! In fact, it was a logical response when so many people started to say, "I'll pray for you," and automatically I said to myself, "And what about you? Why don't you do that too?" Now I'm reading the Psalms as prayer. I must say, some of them are "difficult" and others are "just perfect." Anyway, I'm making my way along this path too. If you have suggestions, let me know!

Magda / February 5, 2013

We're doing well, and now we've returned to normal routines after the week of vacation in Austria. The month of January was complicated by some sores on my head that, fortunately, are now healed.

I would like to come and spend some time with you again to talk about the Psalms. I'm finishing them—I'm on 142 and need to know how to continue. Some of them I find to be very good, and others are much harder for me; and I've discovered that I already knew some of the verses!

February 13, 2013

Dear family and friends:

I successfully passed my five-month ITV *[Inspecció Tècnica de Vehicles, a mandated vehicle inspection for technical standards]*, both the lab tests and clinical visit: normal analyses and no clinical evidence of lung problems. I will continue on the "miracle pill" for another month. If there's nothing new, the next CAT scan will be on April 18th.

After resolving the sores on my head and other "owies" secondary to the medication and antibiotics, I really do feel much better. Although not life-threatening problems, I must admit they left me a little low on energy. Nonetheless, I think now I'm an expert on the use of lotions, creams, salves, soaps, shampoos, and herbal remedies.

Now I hope to get a break from the skin problems so I can go with Marc to his "investiture" as secretary general of the International Federation of Societies for Surgery of the Hand (IFSSH) in New Delhi, India.

Thank you for keeping in touch.

Magda

When I met with Magda again, I gave her this list of Psalms for morning, midday, afternoon/evening, and night prayer, just as they are in the Rule of Saint Benedict.[7]

PSALMS FOR DAILY PRAYER

- *To begin the day:*   *95, 3, 67*

- *At mid-morning:*

Sunday	*51, 118, 63*
Monday	*5, 36*
Tuesday	*43, 57*
Wednesday	*64, 65*
Thursday	*88, 90*
Friday	*76, 92*
Saturday	*143*
Every day	*148, 149, 150*

     + Song of Zacharias   Luke 1:68-79
     + Lord's Prayer

- *During the day:*   *119*
  (normally in clusters of 3):   *120-128*

- *Evening:*

Sunday	*110, 111, 112, 113*
Monday	*114, 115, 116-7, 129*
Tuesday	*130, 131, 132, 133*
Wednesday	*135, 136, 137, 138*
Thursday	*139, 140, 141*
Friday	*142, 144, 145(I)*
Saturday	*145(II), 146, 147*

     + Song of Mary (Magnificat) Luke 1:46-56
     + Lord's Prayer

- *Before sleep:*   *4, 91, 134*

     + Song of Simeon   Luke 2:29-32

Ignasi / March 23, 2013

We still have a few things pending that I haven't responded to.

First of all, I am very happy about the results of your checkup. What you said about patience is very important; as with most medicines, it's easy to prescribe a drug and not so easy to take it.

Thank you for your sympathy about the death of Fr. Oriol. For me, personally, he was important because he was my confessor from the time I entered the monastery until just a few months ago. He was, truly, a spiritual father.

I celebrate that you and Marc can travel to the US. That's a good sign, and for you, who are so used to "crossing the pond," it's probably not quite like going to Matadepera,* but almost!

[*Matadepera, where Marc and Magda lived at the time, is close to Terrassa (a city of 200,000), where both of them were born. Especially in the summer, Matadepera has long been an environmental haven for people from Terrassa due to its higher elevation, pine forest, streams, wildlife, and hiking trails.]

March 23, 2013

Dear ones:

Here are the new monthly follow-up results from this week. Both the lab and clinical results are very good and, therefore, I have medication for another month.

Although the medication I am taking seems to be treating my lung well, it does not offer my skin the same consideration, and the reaction to the "miracle drug" is eczema and itchiness. They tell me this is normal and must be treated with corticosteroids, and most of all with patience. Therefore, I am acquiring personal experience with skin conditions and various skin care oils and creams.

The next checkup will be after six months of treatment, with another CAT scan, and will be the definitive test of the treatment. It goes without saying that I'm confident there will be changes with respect to the last one.

I wish you a good Holy Week, and thank you for paying attention to me.

Magda

Magda / April 20, 2013

Many thanks, Ignasi, for the time we shared at our home last evening. This morning Marc and I talked about the good visit we had together and how fortunate we are to have good friends who accompany us on this journey, you among them (the most recent one!).

Ignasi / April 21, 2013

Many thanks to both of you, Magda and Marc. For me it was a very pleasant evening. I've told you this before, but I have the sense that I'm the one who receives the most from our friendship and that I learn more from you. And for this I also give thanks to God.

April 25, 2013

Dear friends and family:

ITV again. . . with CAT. The CAT scan showed that the size of the tumor has stabilized, but now there were no mediastinal nodes, although lymphangitis had increased (qualitative assessment); since I had bronchitis recently, during a trip to Chicago, maybe that contributed to bronchial inflammation (?). The lab tests were good and I feel good and have energy to do things. In fact, my activity level during the month of April was considerable.

My skin is much better, with the invaluable help of small doses of corticosteroids and antihistamines, in addition to the daily oils and other hydrating lotions and creams.

The oncologist says that we'll keep everything the same and that my clinical status is the determining factor. So, another month of the medication and hoping that everything keeps heading in a good direction.

This month was exceptional because of our vacation with our friends in Chicago, shared with Anna and Xavi, and the impressive spectacle of spring with its changing landscapes and gardens. I suppose that now I have more time to observe it and be surprised by it; it happened before, too, but I was always stuck at the hospital without even time to look out the window! It's another positive thing about this illness that I didn't expect . . .

Thank you for paying attention and for your support, which helps me every day.

Magda

Magda / April 29, 2013

As a complement to the printed copy of the *Revista* I brought you, I'm sending you the index for the May issue of the journal. We send this to all subscribers a few days before the print edition becomes available. In this issue, there is an editorial about hypothermia after cardiac arrest, something I remember discussing one of the first times we talked. As I've told you, the electronic edition is much better because the figures are in color and you have simultaneous access to the English and Spanish editions. If you're interested in browsing the articles, you have free access to those with an open-chain icon, but you need a password for the other texts/PDFs. You can use mine.

Simultaneous publication in both languages was one of the objectives I set for myself when I began as editor in chief, and this effort has been recognized by Medline, which now classifies the *Revista Española de Cardiología* as a bilingual journal. We have two copy editors who do magnificent work with the English and make the English texts fresh, agile, and to the point (instead of Spanglish).*

Anyway, that's a small sample of my work, in case you're interested in knowing how I spend my time (and what has saved my mental health over the past seven months, along with the assignments you have given me!). Of course, your current interests are probably pretty far from cardiology because you're not really in the thick of it.

Greetings from "The Editor," Magda

*As Magda wrote in her first email to me, one of the interesting aspects of our conversations was that we could talk about medicine as readily as about spirituality, because we had both areas in common. One aspect of her work as a cardiologist that had recently given her the greatest satisfaction was the

Spanish cardiology journal, *Revista Española de Cardiología,* of which she was named editor in chief in late 2009. In that role, Magda managed to give the journal a higher international profile (the famous "impact factor") than ever before. She focused on two key elements: the journal's bilingual status (high-quality, simultaneous publication in Spanish and in English) and its electronic publication and web presence.

Magda / May 4, 2013

You told me that our patients are well under control and that's good news.* Tomorrow I will come to the Conventual Mass with Marc and his mother, and we will stay for lunch. Maybe I could have a look at the patients' vital signs in case we need to make some adjustment.

Let's also plan to meet someday during the week of the 13th to the 17th, if that works for you, to keep my own "spiritual health" moving forward.

*One day in February 2013, F. Hilari Raguer[11] wasn't feeling well and I was called to him. I suspected a myocardial infarction, so we did an electrocardiogram and emailed it to Magda. She confirmed the diagnosis and, while we waited for an ambulance, she sent instructions via WhatsApp as if we were in an emergency ward: Put in an IV, give him this med and that one, monitor his vital signs . . . Her professional reflexes kicked in immediately but, poor me, I could only have given him an aspirin and prayed for the ambulance to arrive quickly. When she learned where they were taking him, Magda immediately activated her spirit of service and, using her network of friends and colleagues at that hospital, kept us informed about the patient's progress. After three days there was a serious complication and I am convinced (we all are, starting with the patient himself) that the monk is still alive thanks to Magda's personal intervention. I explain this because, in addition (Divine Providence again intervenes), this monk had published an edition of the book of Psalms with brief introductions for each one, precisely the book that I had recommended to Magda. From that point on, she monitored this monk's health—and a few others as well. They were "her patients" at Montserrat. I think that being able to continue doing some clinical practice, even tangentially, was good for Magda—but above all, it helped us a lot. As she said in a note to me on May 15, 2013: *"In fact, I think I need them more than they need me . . . they are now my only chance to be a doctor and I miss it very much."*

Magda / May 7, 2013

Today I went walking in the foothills of Sant Llorenç *[very near Matadepera]*, just beyond Vacarisses, and I had Montserrat in front of me all the time, with a splendid view of the mountain, and I thought about the visit on Sunday, which we enjoyed a lot. For my mother-in-law, that was a very special day because for a long time she had wanted to come along, but hesitated to ask us. In addition, she was able to chat with Fr. Josep, which brought back many memories for her. His sister Montserrat, who died so young, was her close friend and she has always missed her. When we left on the funicular, I showed her from the car exactly where Cuixà* is (Google Maps, what would we do without it?) and she kept saying how lucky she was to have visited with him at the monastery.

It's curious how everything has been pure coincidence (visiting another monk with heart disease!). My father would say that it is the fruit of Divine Providence and others would say "the world is a handkerchief" *[an idiom meaning "it's a small world"]*. As you saw, my mother-in-law is also a woman with a faith "etched in stone" (I am surrounded!).

What *I* say is that my relationship with your community is changing my life and has become my Prozac. (Don't look for it in the *Vademecum* [Vademecum Académico de Medicamentos, *an authoritative pharmacology handbook*] because it's not listed!)

We'll plan to meet again for a checkup . . .

PS: Can you send me the link to connect to Vespers? I do not have access via iTunes because the app does not work. Can I access it through your website?

*[Note: *Cuixà, home of Fr. Josep, is the site of a Benedictine monastery founded in the ninth century on the eastern side of the Pyrenees, in what was formerly part of Catalonia and is now French territory. Part of the twelfth-century cloister is now displayed in "The Cloisters Collection" of the Metropolitan Museum of Art in New York City: https://www.metmuseum.org/art/collection/search/470314.]*

Magda / May 12, 2013

I saw during Vespers tonight that another monk has died. I don't know if it was expected, but we send you our sympathies.

Magda / May 18, 2013

Although it's noon, I'm just getting myself started. We are in Isil, in the Pyrenees. It's cold and we have snow close by, but everything has burst into a bright green, the river is flowing spectacularly, and the few forest flowers that dare to come out give a beautiful color to its banks . . . between rain squalls.

As always, thanks for Thursday afternoon. I have many friends but none with your availability to talk about EVERYTHING, and this helps me in a way that is difficult to explain.

One question stayed "in my inkwell," about the *Introduction to the Psalms* by Saint Athanasius.[10] In the conclusions, there is a reference to how the Psalms should be sung and the Rule of Saint Benedict is cited (I think it's #81—I don't have the book in front of me), where it says *"Mens nostra concordet voci nostrae."* Does this have anything to do with the fact that, when monks read in church, most of you have a tone of voice and a way of speaking that it is "typical of the monks of Montserrat"? On the other hand, I can't quite link Saint Athanasius (I think you told me he was from the fourth century) to the Rule of Saint Benedict from the seventh or eighth century. Or maybe I've just gotten it all mixed up . . .

The Noguera River in spring

Ignasi / May 20, 2013

I have had a very full weekend and now I am a bit calmer (Father Abbot is out all week and therefore I don't have the regular meetings with him).

With regard to note #81 of the Letter to Marcellinus on the Psalms, it refers to an important topic in the monastic tradition of prayer (which can apply to all Christians). We start with biblical anthropology, which identifies three areas in the human being: the body, the soul (the psychological, emotional dimension), and the spirit (the spiritual dimension). These three areas are inseparable, always together but never confused. In prayer they can be identified with some ease. When we pray, on the one hand we use the body: we put ourselves in a certain position, we speak or sing—they say that even if we pray alone in silence, we move our tongues imperceptibly, as if we want to pronounce what we are reading. We add our psychology: we may be happy or sad, energetic or tired, etc. And there is also our spiritual dimension: this is where prayer reaches its peak.

According to the monastic tradition, in prayer the order of these areas is from the body to the spirit (and not vice versa, as we ourselves might spontaneously assume). In other words, one begins to recite psalms, we might say, in a "mechanical" way, without understanding everything (the soul, psychology, intelligence still participate very little, and the spirit may still be far away from prayer). Little by little, those words that we say begin to impregnate our interior selves and the prayer becomes unveiled in the spirit.

When Saint Athanasius wrote, "He should take what they (the Psalms) say about each of these situations, present it to the Lord, and say it as if the words were written precisely so that he would say them; in this way, his spirit is in accord with what has been written" *[Note: Fr. Ignasi's own translation from Greek]*, that is what he was saying.

Two centuries later, Saint Benedict says the same thing with this phrase that has become a classic: "Let the monks pray in their hearts in such a way that their minds (or we could also say their spirits) are in harmony with their voices" *[see RB 19.7]*.

Obviously, between Saint Athanasius (fourth century) and Saint Benedict (sixth century), there was no direct relationship. They were separated by two centuries, two cultures (Hellenistic, Roman), two languages (Greek, Latin), and two landscapes (Alexandria, South-Central Italy), but they had in common the Christian faith and the monastic tradition (Saint Benedict copied from both the Eastern and Western monastic traditions), and therefore agreed about this order in the learning of monastic wisdom: from the body to the psychology *[the mind]* to finally reach the spirit.

The fact that in Montserrat we all end up reading and singing in a very similar way has, I think, more to do with the fact of living in community. The community tends to create a style, a way to do things to which we all adapt ourselves.

I have been following the emails with Brother Sergi about the contacts in the US and the subject of the "endowment fund." Thank you very much for your cooperation and your efforts.*

As for the Mass on June 29ᵗʰ *[for Magda's 60ᵗʰ birthday]*, I reserved the Saint Joseph Chapel (next to the Cambril) at five in the afternoon (the Cambril has a group scheduled at that time). The Saint Joseph Chapel is small, but ten people will fit well. If you think we will be more, we will look for another place.

It was funny that you said you can talk about EVERYTHING with me. That hadn't occurred to me. There is a classical author (Terence, I think) who said: "I am human, and everything that is human interests me." And Paul VI, when he went to the *[United Nations]* General Assembly, said he came in the name of an institution that "is an expert on humanity." I would like to be like that.

Thanks to you, Magda, once again. How beautiful it must be in Isil these days!

*Another area in which Magda helped us was that of the Escolania. At that time, we were thinking about the possibility of raising funds in the United States, as had been recommended to us in several contexts. Magda's experience with the world and culture of the US was of great value to us.

May 20, 2013

Dear friends and family:

As you already know, on June 29th—God willing—I'll be 60 years old!

Traditionally, birthdays are celebrated with more intensity when they are especially significant (coming of age, entering a new decade, etc.). In my case, the change in decade comes along with my delight at having reached this milestone despite my personal battle with a "pulmonary invader" that has radically changed my daily life over the past eight months. Therefore, I think this is reason for satisfaction and joy and it should be celebrated with all of you who love me and have been at my side during this difficult and different stage in my life.

Having already announced that the party would be on June 29th, however, I realize that date coincides with a macro-concert by Lluís Llach and the call for our own Catalan state in Europe. I cannot compete with this important event, nor do I want to. To avoid making you choose, I have decided to have the party the night before, the eve of Sant Pere,* the 28ᵗʰ of June. I'll be expecting you.

Magda

[*Sant Pere = Feast Day of Saint Peter, the main summer festival in Terrassa, celebrated for a week and including many popular traditions on the weekend of the Feast Day.]

Magda / May 21, 2013

Thank you for agreeing to come to my birthday celebration, Ignasi. I'm very happy you'll be there. You're a "special friend" (*without* even having "a partner"!), and thank you, too, for the whole explanation of the three levels of prayer. I must be on the first floor trying to get to the second floor—the psychological part—somehow, but I hope that if I can just work out enough I'll make it up to the third floor (spirit).

Even though you're more an urban guy and now I know you really like the sea, we'd like you to come to Isil some day(s) this summer and, if you want, you could bring your mother along. I promise not to make you climb any mountain peaks—my current lung capacity is more appropriate for "granny walks" along the river (also beautiful!!).

Magda / May 22, 2013

Verses 10-14 of Psalm 65 describe Isil this weekend. The psalmist must have written it here!

Ignasi / May 22, 2013

"O Lord our God, you provide us with bountiful goodness"
(v. 6)* . . . Isil must be so beautiful.

[*Translated directly from the Catalan Bible verse.]

> The verses Magda sent from Psalm 65 became my contribution
> when her daughter Anna asked for letters to include in Magda's
> 60th birthday album. The text I submitted, with my signature,
> was the following:

⁹ You care for the land and water it;
    you enrich it abundantly.
The streams of God are filled with water
    to provide the people with grain,
    for so you have ordained it.
¹⁰ You drench its furrows and level its ridges;
    you soften it with showers and bless its crops.
¹¹ You crown the year with your bounty,
    and your carts overflow with abundance.
¹² The grasslands of the wilderness overflow;
    the hills are clothed with gladness.
¹³ The meadows are covered with flocks
    and the valleys are mantled with grain;
    they shout for joy and sing.
                            Psalm 65:9-13

> From the same Psalm, verse 6: O Lord our God, you provide
> us with bountiful goodness . . .
>   " . . . that was Isil this weekend. The psalmist must have
>   written it there!" (Magda)
> I don't know where the psalmist was when he wrote this
> psalm. But I'm sure that He who inspired the psalmist also cre-
> ated Isil. Everything has come from His hands: the human
> heart and the wonders of creation. And everything is called to
> return to Him in Jesus Christ.
>
> *Per molts anys,** Magda!
>
> *[*Literally, "for many years"—used for Happy Birthday/Anni-
> versary and other congratulations.]*

Magda / May 22, 2013

Ignasi, we will not come to Salve at noon because my friends got confused about the schedule. Now it is clear that we will meet with Brother Sergi on Friday afternoon at 5:30, at the *Escolania*, and then they will stay for Vespers and Salve and overnight at Cisneros *[Hotel Abat Cisneros, within the abbey complex]*.

I'll go back home because I will spend the weekend with Gemma, one of my sisters, in Palafrugell. Marc goes to the Mayo Clinic this Thursday, and I'd rather not be alone Saturday and Sunday. Before this illness, I loved being alone at home and doing whatever I wanted, but now I need to be with someone because the company helps me to "control the brain." Sometimes I don't recognize myself, a Type-A personality, continuously looking for companionship . . . Ah, and Monday, another onco appointment . . .

We have never talked about it directly, but I hope that you are one of those who are praying for me, that you have me "on your prayer list," as Sister Margaret says.

Magda / May 28, 2013

I'm on the Sant Jeroni trail *[the highest peak on the mountain of Montserrat]* with a friend from Hospital Clínic. We'll come down for lunch. Can we say hello to you and maybe have coffee?

Ignasi / May 28, 2013

Yes, sure. OK. I'll come to Cisneros at 3:15.

Sometimes we had "informal" conversations, like this day when Magda came to Montserrat with another doctor from her hospital. They were walking around the mountain and stayed for lunch, and I joined them when it came to desserts and coffee. These first months of illness, when she felt quite well, allowed Magda to rediscover the beauty of the little things and of the many marvels of each day, which normally—as busy as we are—go unnoticed. In this case, it was the beauty of the mountain of Montserrat in a splendid spring.

Magda / May 28, 2013

Hello again, and thanks for your company during dessert.

The Montserrat walk today was a powerful balm for the news from yesterday's tests: the tumor markers have increased. I have not yet been able to talk with the oncologist about it because they were missing two tests; during the visit we still did not have those results. I downloaded them myself yesterday afternoon. By WhatsApp, she told me that this was not a reason to change the treatment, but I cannot help thinking there are indications that the disease is less controlled . . .

Yesterday I started taking fluoxetine (a mild antidepressant) in order to live through what is to come (if it comes!) with some peace of mind.

I realize that for eight months now I have been like this and, in the absence of an end point, I think it's starting to weigh on me. As I said to you once, there are moments when I almost do not recognize myself. I am very lucky to have Marc, family, and friends—among which you play an important role. We don't train for adversity, so a major jolt like this requires a lot of "digestion."

Sorry this message is a little grim, but it's good for me to share it. The friend you met today is another "listening ear" that helps me a lot.

I'm going to the Palau[12] to enjoy Händel.

Ignasi / May 28, 2013

In fact, I wanted to ask if you had news about the lab tests, but I didn't dare (I told you that I'm very shy).

I understand your situation, and can comprehend that it must be a heavy weight. On the other hand, we all have the right to "turn to mush" sometimes, and this also humanizes us. Tell your friend that I have already greeted Brother E. from her sister. He was very happy, and when I told him that they miss him very much, he even blushed. I was happy to meet her. She is a person who inspires confidence and sweetness. I mean, I would calmly put myself in her hands, if I needed medical care.

Enjoy the concert!

PS: Of course you are on my "prayer list" ever since that day in September last year in the reception area. Someday, if you think about it, pray for me too (we all need it), and now your prayers have more specific weight (one day I'll tell you what I mean).

Magda / May 29, 2013

I just talked to the oncologist, who said that the markers were not important, the increase was very slight, and they can increase due to other types of associated conditions (smoking, bronchitis, etc.). Therefore, what guides the treatment, apart from clinical symptoms, is only the CAT scan. They will repeat it in July but until then, we continue the same as before.

Now I think that, in addition to brushing up on cardiology and forensic medicine,* you will soon understand about lung adenocarcinomas! And all thanks to my stubbornness about sharing my pains . . . and some joys.

> *During this period, I did the "recognitio" of the remains of the martyred monks who were to be beatified in Tarragona in mid-October. I had told Magda that, as a student, the only specialization I would never have thought of ever doing was forensic medicine!

The concert was exceptional, the second gift of yesterday (the other being the time at Montserrat). There was an Italian baroque quintet, and Xavier Sabata sang very well, with a lot of expression; we enjoyed it very much.

You can be sure that I will pray for you, intrigued about the "special weight."

A more peaceful and encouraged *abraçada*

Magda / June 3, 2013

I'll come up tomorrow afternoon, and I'll stay for Vespers if you have time to talk a little more. At what time are confessions?

When reading Psalm 92, v. 11 ("and you lift my forehead, like the buffalo's*, you anoint it with new oil"), I cannot stop thinking about the Hindu ritual that we saw in Nepal. Obviously, it's not a buffalo but a skinny cow . . . . I wonder what kind of link there is between the two . . .

Hindu ritual in Nepal

Ignasi / June 3, 2013

In principle, the time for confessions is 12:00 to 1:00, but in the afternoon you can also find a confessor. Concerning Psalm 92, it only refers to buffalo*: "lifts the forehead" (literally "the horn") = gives me strength to defeat the enemies.

[*No English translation uses the word "buffalo." For example: "You have exalted my horn like that of the wild ox" (Psalm 92:10, New Revised Standard Version, Catholic Edition) or "You have given me the strength of a wild ox" (Psalm 92:11, New American Bible, Revised Edition).]

Magda / June 5, 2013

Yesterday you totally amazed me with the organization of my visit. Approaching confession (something I had been "lugging around" without knowing how or where to deal with it) was very delicate for me. Fr. Lluís is an exemplar of humanity and you find yourself telling him about your life as if you have known him forever; but above all, avoiding that "wooden box with bars" *[iconic confessional booth]* was the definitive master stroke!

My researcher mentality makes me wonder about the difference between being a monk from Montserrat and being a "regular" priest. I suppose that like everything in life, nothing is easy or just handed to you, so I intuit that there is hard personal work involved in achieving such openness and *bonhomie.*

I am really excited and very happy to be able to visit often and find you all "always prepared"!—like the Scouts!

By the way, we still have a pending question about "physics": the specific weight of my prayers for you . . . I find it hard to understand that there are different "rankings"; I don't know how prayer could be "weighed" . . . maybe this thinking is a little irreverent but I am very intrigued.*

By the way, I went to play tennis and I think I feel a little less tired (now I am devoting myself to evaluating "feelings." As my grandmother said, "A person with no work to do combs the cat"!). *[Note: This is a Catalan idiom, "Qui no te feina el gat pentina."]*

And I'll end by saying that I will never be able to thank you for everything you are doing for me and how much it is helping me at this stage.

*[*This question was discussed in person and therefore not documented. In response to the translator's query, Ignasi explained: "I am convinced that the prayers of one who is suffering are more profound—maybe even more 'valid'—than*

the prayer of someone with no problems at all. This is because someone who suffers can more fully identify with Jesus Christ, and our prayer is indeed prayer to the extent that it identifies with the prayers of Jesus."]

Magda / June 17, 2013

Yesterday I wanted to watch Vespers on the Internet but there was no sound. I suppose you know that, but just in case . . . there was only the image.

I would also like to know what days you will come to Isil so that we can be making plans; remember that your mother will also be welcome!

I continue to feel well, "working" a lot; tomorrow I am on the committee for a doctoral thesis defense, and I am preparing a couple of lectures as well as the journal. I cannot complain . . . I guess "my patients" at the monastery are fine; greet them from me.

Can I ask how many monks you are, total? I would like to bring something for you on the 29th.

Ignasi / June 17, 2013

Thanks for the information about the transmission over the Internet. In recent days there have been technical problems. (One day I'll have to share my thoughts about this technology stuff.)

About your patients, they are very well. "No news, good news."

In total, in the community, living at Montserrat, we are 55 monks.

As for the visit to Isil with my mother, I still don't know when I'm going to have a vacation because it depends on my sister/sister-in-law, who have not yet told me anything, and other things at Montserrat. I had imagined a day trip to Isil (I know it's very little, but it's better than nothing). If you can tell me which days you will be there in July/August, I can look to find a date.

I'm glad you're working hard.

I am off to Vespers now.

June 28, 2013

Text read by Magda at her 60th birthday celebration

Good evening and welcome!

Sixty years ago, it was a stormy night when I decided to be born after almost two days of labor. So, I arrived in the world with a slightly restless spirit—and this characteristic has defined me as a person. This evening we're a large group of family, friends, and colleagues. My parents, far from shrinking away from the difficult experience of that first birth, just kept right on having children, and that has given me a large family of more than 30 people; and we have really good times together. On the other hand, when Marc decided that I was the woman of his dreams (at least until now!), I joined another large family, and now when both families are together there are more than 50 of us.

I am also very lucky to have many friends. Some of us have shared our lives for 45 years, and other more recent friends have shared unforgettable experiences like hiking the GR *[Great Route through the Pyrenees]*, gastronomical excursions, hiking in Sant Maurici National Park and all over the Pallars Sobirà, etc.

After 35 years, our friends from medical school still get together. Just recently, I had a happy reunion with my three friends and colleagues from the first years of residency in internal medicine.

There is also a group of colleagues here, among them my cardiology professors and some students who are now great professionals, and the nurses who are fundamental to the life of a hospital, and the people with whom I have done research for so many years.

I also can't forget my faithful and incombustible tennis partner, Mercè. And some of you have even come from far away to be here, like Isabel from Palma *[Mallorca]*; Roger and his daughters Miranda and Lucinda from Finland—thank you, girls, for being here tonight; and my indispensable friend and manuscript editor, Elaine, from Minnesota.

All of you who are here have helped me ensure that my life continues to have meaning, full of hikes, breakfasts, suppers, cafés, theatres, poems, psalms, etc.

That is why it makes me so happy today that you have taken the time to celebrate with me as I achieve this goal of reaching my 60th birthday! Thank you for being here, and I hope we all enjoy this evening together.

Applause for Magda's 60th birthday remarks

Magda / July 6, 2013

I would like to know how Fr. Hilari's first "job" in Barcelona is going. Can you give me his email address? I suppose he won't mind if I write him; I would offer him the possibility to write to me if he has any questions or some specific problem.

Marc agrees that you have to come to Isil for two whole days, or we will not be able to enjoy your company. Therefore, it would be ideal if you come for dinner on Thursday, August 1st, and leave Saturday evening, the 3rd. Don't worry about the extra work; I'll leave things for you to do. . . . The house is designed for visitors and friends are always welcome.

We are in Andorra, in a hotel with views of the mountains that are now covered by clouds, and Psalm 147 is "perfect." I have continued with your prayer plan and I am starting to know some verses by heart. . . .

Thank you as always for the time we shared. . . . How lucky I am to have connected with you!

Una abraçada, and get some rest after so many "short courses" this week.

Ignasi / July 7, 2013

Isil Project: This week I'll see Father Abbot and we will look at the calendar. Yesterday I spoke on the phone with my mother, and the only thing that worries her is the altitude. (She has a pacemaker and a coronary stent, and when she has to go anywhere she always asks if it is very high altitude.) I told her that it's no problem and that my friends are doctors (a traumatologist and cardiologist, to be more precise), so she laughed and said: "Ah! So I can get sick with no worries!" Therefore, everything looks like we will come up to Isil, if God wills, for a couple or three days. I will confirm it.

Thank you, too, for the moments shared. I can say the same thing: how lucky I am to have reconnected with you.

July 15, 2013

Dear friends:
   Today at 2:00 p.m. I had a CAT scan and the radiologist has told me:
       - that the tumor has grown;
       - that my right lung has collapsed again;

- that we need to look at the liver to rule out metastasis.

I was lucky to be able to speak with the oncologist immediately, and I already have an abdominal ultrasound scheduled for tomorrow morning, and other tests (among them new biopsies to understand if these cells that are growing now have some different mutation). The advantage of having worked in that hospital for more than thirty years is that everything is getting done at a rapid rate, and I appreciate it.

The good news is that they're letting me leave for Salzburg next Monday with the family, as we had planned, while waiting for the results to know which treatments are best suited for this new stage.

Well, after winning the battle for the first 10 months, which I got through very well, I now have to roll up my sleeves to start the second (and possibly the last) battle, to finally win the war. That came out a little "warrior-like" but it takes a fighting spirit to move forward. I am very grateful to everyone who is being so attentive and giving me so much encouragement.

I love you so much!
Magda

Magda / July 15, 2013

I received your WhatsApp, but I can answer more easily by email.

You will see the small report I have written for my family and close friends, which includes you. Nothing that I explain there changes the plans for your visit to Isil August 1–3; for me, that would be the worst that could happen. It is possible that if the treatment decision is chemotherapy it will not begin until the second week of August. In fact, as you saw yesterday, I feel really good and have no symptoms.

It is a new "trial by fire" that I hope to be able to face with the help of so many friends and many prayers. In a moment of "hooliganism," I've thought, "God must get tired of so many people praying for me, so maybe he should make a gesture of 'good faith' and just heal me once and for all!" I am sure that thinking like this borders on irreverence, but it's how I feel. . . . I will have to further intensify the reading of Psalms and understand better what it means to say "Your will be done" . . .

I hope you have an appropriate reflection for a "difficult day."

Ignasi / July 15, 2013

I had no reflection prepared, of course. First of all, I fully share your hooligan thinking. Rather, it seems to me a clear example of how you have perfectly understood the language of the psalmists and the frankness with which they speak to God. A phrase attributed to Saint Teresa of Avila has come into my head, in which she says to God something like: "I'm not surprised that you have so few followers, if this is how you treat those who choose you."*

Now I have even more desire to come to Isil. I keep praying to see if all together we can "bore" God, as the widow did the judge in a parable (Luke 18:1-8).

Una abraçada from your "long-lost brother"

[*"*Dear Lord, if this is how You treat Your friends, it is no wonder You have so few!*" reportedly said by Saint Teresa of Avila as she was bucked off her horse into a river on the way to visit one of her monasteries.]

Magda / July 17, 2013

Yesterday an abdominal echo confirmed multiple metastases in both lobes of the liver.

Tomorrow, they'll do a new biopsy of the tumor to see if another mutation can be identified. These are tough days that I am living through with quite a sense of peace.

On Monday we go to Salzburg with part of the Heras clan. I hope I can keep up with the pace.

Ignasi / July 17, 2013

I keep praying and thinking about you very often, and Marc and Anna too. I have Psalm 42 in front of me, especially verse 11: "Why, my soul, are you downcast? Why so disturbed within me? Put your hope in God, for I will yet praise him, my Savior and my God."

Magda / July 18, 2013

I read it yesterday (it was on the schedule), and I identified with it. Thank you for sharing it. Today it's 88 and 90, also very suitable! The other one that is good now is 13 . . .

Next summer I will be able to teach a course on the Psalms if I just apply myself a bit more! Now at 11:00, the biopsy! Think of me.

Ignasi / July 18, 2013

I prayed especially for you at the Conventual Mass. I hope they didn't make you suffer too much during the biopsy.

Magda / July 18, 2013

I'm already awake. Propofol (a sedative) works wonders. They're watching my blood pressure and I'm hypotensive, so they're worried because I'm at 86/40, but I feel good. Now I need some luck so they find "attackable" cells. Thank you for the Conventual prayers.

Ignasi / July 22, 2013

Dear Magda: Much happiness on your saint's day![13]

Magda / July 22, 2013

Thank you very much, Ignasi. Actually, instead of leaving for Austria I spent the morning at Hospital Clínic where I had a thoracic puncture to evacuate 1100 ml. of fluid, and now I feel much better. Tomorrow we will take the plane to Salzburg, where we'll arrive at the same time as the rest of the Heras "troupe" (17 in all) and we will join the party. Really, yesterday evening I was very dyspneic and I felt awful. This morning I saturated at 92![14]

Next Monday, I will have the new treatment plan and I want to start it to see if I'm going to feel good again. As you can see, a different sort of "gift" for my saint's day. When we see you in Isil we'll have topics of conversation!

Una abraçada

Ignasi / July 22, 2013

Omigosh!!! . . . and me congratulating you for your saint's day.

Magda / July 22, 2013

Who said that the ways of the Lord are inscrutable? Anyway, it will be an unforgettable saint's day!

Psalm 88

LORD, you are the God who saves me;
    day and night I cry out to you.
2 May my prayer come before you;
    turn your ear to my cry.

3 I am overwhelmed with troubles
    and my life draws near to death.
4 I am counted among those who go down to the pit;
    I am like one without strength.
5 I am set apart with the dead,
    like the slain who lie in the grave,
whom you remember no more,
    who are cut off from your care.

6 You have put me in the lowest pit,
    in the darkest depths.
7 Your wrath lies heavily on me;
    you have overwhelmed me with all your waves.
8 You have taken from me my closest friends
    and have made me repulsive to them.
I am confined and cannot escape;
9   my eyes are dim with grief.

I call to you, LORD, every day;
    I spread out my hands to you.
10 Do you show your wonders to the dead?
    Do their spirits rise up and praise you?
11 Is your love declared in the grave,
    your faithfulness in Destruction?
12 Are your wonders known in the place of darkness,
    or your righteous deeds in the land of oblivion?

> [13] But I cry to you for help, LORD;
>   in the morning my prayer comes before you.
> [14] Why, LORD, do you reject me
>   and hide your face from me?
> [15] From my youth I have suffered and been close to death;
>   I have borne your terrors and am in despair.
> [16] Your wrath has swept over me;
>   your terrors have destroyed me.
> [17] All day long they surround me like a flood;
>   they have completely engulfed me.
> [18] You have taken from me friend and neighbor—
>   darkness is my closest friend.

Magda / July 30, 2013

It's decided that I'll start intravenous chemotherapy. Now you can ask your boss to "make it easy on me." The plan for the days at Isil goes ahead as proposed. Maybe you'll have to spend time with somebody who's a little "woozy" at times, but I promise to behave myself. We will have very tranquil days because my capacity for exercise is below minimal, but I really want to see you in Isil.

Fr. Hilari Raguer[11] / July 30, 2013

I hope that yesterday you came out of the doctor's office in good spirits and hopeful. But we must continue praying Psalm 13.

I call it "the psalm of the angry believer," with its fourfold hammering on "how long . . . how long . . . how long . . . how long . . . " When he says "how long," he means that it has been a long time and the end is not in sight. In Revelation 6:10, the souls of the martyrs call out: "How long, Lord, before you will do justice?" God asks them to wait a little, until the number of martyrs who are still missing is completed, but does not say how many are missing.

In the Psalms, some want to eat à la carte and select a few fervent and devout psalms, doing away with those they find violent or difficult. But the Holy Spirit was completely right to inspire some that fit us like rings to our fingers when we do not understand the way God is working. Disrespectful psalms, protest songs, which God places in our mouths so that we make them our own when we are ill. When I am healthy and I feel fervent, I don't need the Psalms.

In the Psalms, there is a lot about enemies. Some girls on retreat in a French monastery, who were scratching the surface of the Psalms for the first time, told a nun: "We did not know you had so many enemies!" In Psalm 13, the only enemy is death, and I encourage you not to surrender, not as a doctor to the illness of your patients, nor personally as a patient yourself.

Psalm 13

¹ How long, LORD? Will you forget me forever?
  How long will you hide your face from me?
² How long must I wrestle with my thoughts
  and day after day have sorrow in my heart?
  How long will my enemy triumph over me?
³ Look on me and answer, LORD my God.
  Give light to my eyes, or I will sleep in death,
⁴ and my enemy will say, "I have overcome him,"
  and my foes will rejoice when I fall.
⁵ But I trust in your unfailing love;
  my heart rejoices in your salvation.
⁶ I will sing the LORD's praise,
  for he has been good to me.

Magda / July 31, 2013

Response to Fr. Hilari Raguer's letter of the day before

Today I begin regular chemotherapy (in a vein) because in the analyses that have been done they could not find any indication that some type of pill would work well. Although it is a treatment I don't really "look forward to," I am energized because I have to improve and this gives me a chance!

Thank you very much for your comments on Psalm 13 —as I said, my "current favorite." It's true that it seems like a protest song we sang at the end of the '70s from American folk music.

I will be very grateful if you continue to think about me and pray for me.

Magda / August 18, 2013

Today I hiked to the Chapel of *[Our Lady of]* the Snows, above Borén—little by little, but I managed to climb to 150 meters. I'm euphoric! And I no longer have the cough. Now I'm ready for the second round! I give many thanks to God because I feel "like myself" again.

On the path to
Nostra Senyora de les Neus

Ignasi / August 18, 2013

Alleluia! I'm glad with you, Magda. I went to say Mass in the monastery of Saint Cecilia for the group of second-year ESO students (who will now be the oldest group in the *Escolania*). A Polish couple from Krakow joined us with two children. At the beginning of the Mass, to break the ice, I said to the schoolchildren: "A family from Krakow is joining us . . . and by the way, what does this name, Krakow, make you think of?" I, of course, thought of Pope John Paul II, and they, on the other hand, the TV3 program![15] (Ha ha.) They looked at me with ???? on their faces and I realized that I am an "altar-piece" *[out of date since Vatican II]*. . . . In short, have a good Sunday and give my greetings to Marc.

Magda / August 18, 2013

That's a great anecdote! I can imagine their faces thinking about the characters that appear in the program. I think JP II must be waaaaay far from their thoughts—and maybe they haven't even heard of him! Certainly, connecting with kids that age requires close contact with them that you probably don't have! Thank you for sharing the story.

Magda / August 22, 2013

Response to a letter from Fr. Hilari Raguer

Many thanks for thinking about me and "accompanying me" in these difficult times. I am very happy about the good news I got yesterday. I am now receiving the second dose of chemotherapy, which will take until five o'clock this afternoon. The first treatment, apart from the side effects, improved my physical symptoms a lot, and this also makes me optimistic.

By the way, this morning I read Psalms 88 and 90 and today my spirit was far from 88! I did not have any burned-out fuses—I have a lot of hope.

Magda / August 29, 2013

The main reason for this message is to ask a question about donating paintings to the museum at Montserrat. When we meet on the 3rd, we can discuss it in more detail.

Roger (an English friend living in Finland whom you met at my 60th) has an extensive collection of paintings by Jacint Morera, a painter from Terrassa who settled in Calella. He has the idea of giving one of the paintings (Last Supper in Cadaquès) to my parents in appreciation for so many years of friendship and good hospitality, with the idea that they can offer it to the Museum of Montserrat, due to their long relationship with the monastery.

The important question is: What are the requirements to accept this type of donation? Are you very selective and you just want certain types of paintings? Recommendations? Suggestions? I have offered to ask these questions directly for Roger because it is easy for me to do, but I am copying him.

I had many fewer problems with this second batch of chemo, but I received only 80% of the dose because they thought I had experienced excessive toxicity. Tomorrow I have the CAT scan (always a complicated day!), but I'm excited because I feel good.

How are "my patients"? I guess they must be stable. In any case, I will arrange to see them some day in September. We'll see you on the 3rd!

Magda / September 3, 2013

Congratulations on the 25th anniversary of your profession of monastic vows, and congratulations on your loyalty to this vocation.

As you know, this past year you have been a fundamental pillar for us *[Magda, Marc, and daughter Anna]*, and we can never thank you enough. We believe that your interest in staying in touch with medicine also plays a role in this relationship, helping us find some shared interests and also allowing my modest collaboration to help you with some specific problems.

It is traditional to give gifts on important anniversaries. We have been thinking about it and decided to give you a sample of our scientific activity, which is an important part of life for Marc, Anna, and me; you too have given us important texts that have helped us grow in other aspects of life. We do not want you to see it as our self-promotion, but rather as sharing our daily activities with you a bit more. In addition, Marc, the artist *[and guitarist]* of the family, has included a recording made more than 30 years ago by a group called Registre 23. Many of the songs are based on poems by Miquel Martí i Pol and other Catalan poets. You can tell that it was recorded "on a shoestring," but at that time digital recording was unknown.

Per molts anys [For many years] may we continue to enjoy this friendship.

Magda / September 4, 2013

I hope that yesterday's celebration *[25 years of monastic vows]* ended as well as it began in the morning. Was there anything special in the afternoon?

I promised Fr. Joan Maria that I will be there on the 10th for the lab tests and echocardiogram. I greeted Fr. Josep, and Fr. Hilari and his sisters. If it's a good time for you to spend some time with me after those medical visits, tell me if you prefer that I come in the morning or afternoon. It's all the same to me.

Ignasi / September 4, 2013

Thanks Magda. Yesterday went very well. In the afternoon we didn't do anything special. I stayed for a while with my family. I showed them the library and my 17-year-old nephew, an athlete and no lover of studying, made one of those undiplomatic faces typical of adolescents: "Uffff, books!!! Couldn't you show us anything else, Unk?"

Thank you for your gift. I found it very original. As for meeting on the 10th, it's good for me in either the morning (except 11 to 12) or afternoon.

Magda / September 4, 2013

You should have shown your nephew the gym and the pool too . . . he would have thought that he has a "really cool" uncle. If it's OK I will come to visit the monks at 9:30 on the 10th, and after Conventual Mass I would like to have some time to chat with you. This could change if the oncologist, whom I will see on the 9th, has other plans for me (I hope not).

> Indeed, on September 10th, Magda came to Montserrat. During the visit with "her patients," her cell phone interrupted her. I was with her in the office.
>
> At first, from the questions she asked, I thought she was talking about a patient at Hospital Clínic, but I quickly realized that

she was talking about herself! They were giving her the results of the bone scintigraphy that had been done a few days before: bone metastases.

I remember the serenity and firmness with which she received the news. When she hung up, she continued the visit with the professionalism that characterized her.

I asked her to stay for lunch.

Magda / September 10, 2013

Thank you for having "put up with me" after the news from the hospital and for your company during lunch. I needed a listening ear and, as always, you were there!

If you have time, please send me the new reading suggestions that you commented on. Today I find that Psalms 6 and 88 —as Fr. Hilari says "for when your fuses burn out"—are the ones that are best for my mood. I went to see my parents and explained the news to them gently. My advantage is that externally I am in very good shape and I want to do things. My parents perceive this as a good sign; they don't care that I need a different chemo for some spots on my bones because they see me as active and happy and because they trust that modern medicine has solutions for everything!

Marc will be home soon and we will go to dinner in Barcelona. This was a birthday gift certificate that we had decided to use today, and we will still go because I think it's best to continue living a life that has the maximum "normality" possible, although if the news were better we would celebrate it more. . . but maybe we also need to continue celebrating the will to go on. By the way, in this regard, the "grace" that we talked about today also must play a good role . . .

Psalm 6

LORD, do not rebuke me in your anger
    or discipline me in your wrath.
² Have mercy on me, LORD, for I am faint;
    heal me, LORD, for my bones are in agony.
³ My soul is in deep anguish.
    How long, LORD, how long?

⁴ Turn, LORD, and deliver me;
    save me because of your unfailing love.
⁵ Among the dead no one proclaims your name.
    Who praises you from the grave?

⁶ I am worn out from my groaning.

All night long I flood my bed with weeping
    and drench my couch with tears.
⁷ My eyes grow weak with sorrow;
    they fail because of all my foes.
⁸ Away from me, all you who do evil,
    for the LORD has heard my weeping.
⁹ The LORD has heard my cry for mercy;
    the LORD accepts my prayer.
¹⁰ All my enemies will be overwhelmed with shame and
    anguish;
    they will turn back and suddenly be put to shame.

Summer in Isil

Ignasi / September 15, 2013

Last Thursday they were doing maintenance tasks on our computer services and that's why it said the email had not been received. Actually, I did get it.

What happened was that I spent all day in Tarragona and until now have not had a moment to answer your emails and messages.

I also received the copy of your email to Roger, which is a delight of clarity and concise expression, with a remarkable balance between assertiveness and engagement. (I would now digress about how this must be the result of years and years of excellent clinical practice, but I'll let it go so as not to tire you.)

Here are the references for the gospel texts on the resurrection of Jesus:

Gospel according to Saint Matthew chapters 26–28
Gospel according to Saint Mark chapters 14–16
Gospel according to Saint Luke chapters 22–24
Gospel according to Saint John chapters 13–21

I also copied out the Lord's Prayer beginning at the end. It may seem like an artificial and somewhat awkward exercise, but I think it helps to rediscover the content of the most well-known prayer, and it can be a good way to deepen the relationship with God the Father. And, as I always say in these things, if it works for you, fantastic—and if not, then let it go. No problem.

But deliver us from evil
and lead us not into temptation.
As we forgive those who trespass against us,
forgive us our trespasses,
Give us this day our daily bread.
Thy will be done on earth, as it is in heaven.
Thy kingdom come.
Our Father who art in heaven, hallowed be thy name.

I hope these days in Isil have gone well. The landscape must be fantastic.

Magda / September 16, 2013

These four days in Isil with Marc have been a pleasure; the landscape is as green as when you were here, because of all the rain. Autumn is appearing timidly in some of the birch leaves, but yellow does not yet dominate the landscape. The roses in the courtyard have blossomed, as well as a couple of hydrangeas, my dream flower of the summer! I guess I should have lived "further north" to enjoy spectacular hydrangeas, but I do not complain about what I have at Isil.

Isil hydrangeas

Yesterday we decided that we would like to spend *La Mercè*[16] at Montserrat to celebrate the first anniversary of our reunion with you. If it is not a red day in the monastery *[i.e., days the monks must be with the Community]*, we would like to have lunch all three together at Cisneros, if your agenda allows it. However, I'm also waiting for a new PET scan on Wednesday or Thursday this week and, depending on the results, will start the new chemotherapy. Therefore, it might be that precisely on that day I will be "a blob" and will have to cancel these plans. What bothers me most about this situation is not being able to control my agenda, which should not surprise you, given my way of being.

> One of the most well-known Catalans living in New York is Dr. Valentí Fuster, and it turned out that Magda was a good friend of his. In fact, she arranged for some monks to spend a summer day in Cardona with Dr. Fuster, his wife, and some family members. It was a very interesting experience for those who did not know him. I was impressed by Dr. Fuster's gentleness toward Magda. At the end, he gave us a copy of one of his latest books, *El círculo de la motivación* [in Spanish; his "circle of motivation" is a spiral composed of four repeating stages].

I read Valentí Fuster's book in one day. Many of his ideas I had heard in lectures and also discussed with him, so the reading was easy. For me, there is a lack of acknowledgment, whether in a footnote or at the end of the book (where he mentions only his family and secretaries) of his collaborators who are moving forward all the projects he describes. It is obvious that he is an idea-generator and that any project, regardless of the cost involved or even if it is strategically difficult, starts with initiative similar to what you witnessed in Cardona. Specifically, the polypill project, described a couple of times in the book, has been led directly and for more than six years by my mentor and friend, Ginés Sanz, whom Marc introduced to you at my birthday party. He is the person who has most influenced my professional and personal life; from him I learned not only a lot of cardiology, but also how to be a good doctor and person.

The same could be said, for example, about the vascular imaging projects. Yes, he talks about his team in the book, but I would have done it differently.

Thank you for telling me that my emails are not a bother. I think being an editor also helps one write better and more clearly and directly. That's what I ask of the authors! Anyway, I will be interested to hear how you associate assertiveness and engagement with being a doctor!

I find the "upside-down" Lord's Prayer rather curious . . . I will work with it a little more and we can talk about it. After "digesting" the news of bone metastases, I feel more optimistic and, since I feel well, I try to take the most positive attitude possible.

Let us know if the plan for the 24th is possible.

Magda / September 19, 2013

I just had good news: the PET captured no bone images and the pulmonary and hepatic involvement has been greatly reduced! My doctors can't explain the disagreement between the two imaging techniques, but for the moment I will follow the same chemotherapy (they wanted to change it because of bone metastases). On the 24th we will celebrate it.

Ignasi / September 19, 2013

Visca! [An enthusiastic cheer in Catalan, literally, "long life!" In Spanish, "Viva!"; in English, maybe "yay!"]

> One of the many areas in which Magda was successful was her cooking. Tasting her dishes or "pastries" reminded me of a phrase attributed to the philosopher Javier Zubiri: "We do not have a body; we are a body." On the 24th, Magda brought me some muffins she had made. She had recycled a box from "The Palace Pantry."[17]

Magda / September 25, 2013

Yesterday I saw your WhatsApp too late to answer.

I love that you like the muffins; they're easy to make and they are good! They are very popular at our house, too.

Certainly yesterday was special, most of all because it marked one year, and the most important dates usually motivate some special reflection.

I was surprised that you remembered so vividly what I said a year ago: I'm only interested in my oncologist and that you teach me to pray! I suppose this summarizes quite well the type of reasoning that I use in the face of problems.

Needless to say, I have done everything I could to follow your instructions and I have drawn from it an inner peace and comfort that I did not think I could have in this situation of vital change. Many times I wonder if I'm doing it well enough, but I think that now I *need* to read Psalms! Curiously, many of your words or phrases have had a healing effect, a balm that you might never have expected.

As we discussed yesterday, I have also learned to think about death, something absolutely unthinkable before the disease; however, I have no desire to die!! I am very happy here, and I know this life. The unknown, even if you think and believe that it will be splendid, is something we can look forward to but, at least for me, it is difficult to understand!

The other thing that I have learned is to have the courage to share fears and worries with family and friends, while still trying not to cause excessive concern for those around me.

This morning, as I woke up and was just thinking everything I have now written down, I was wondering what meaning all of this might have. I don't know whether I need to "pay attention" to some things in my life that I need to change, or to "not look for more feet on the cat" [*referring to a Spanish idiom, "No hay que buscarle cinco patas al gato": "There is no need to look for five feet on a cat."*]. I think it is simply a question of probabilities and it happened to me . . . I don't know if you have any ideas on this.

Well, today my email got a bit dense and "doubt-filled," but looking back over the year encouraged me to write it. I hope that yesterday you were able to end the day well with your friends in the chorale. We did not leave you to yourself for a minute! And today I'm back!

I'm grateful for "the listening ear" that never fails!

Ignasi / September 26, 2013

Yesterday's email really had an effect on me. What you say about the Psalms is much more than I could have imagined a year ago.

I am glad to have served as an instrument to help you discover the prayer of the psalmists, which somehow brings us closer to the person of Jesus and to the way he prayed (second to the Lord's Prayer, of course).

Your reflection on the meaning of what has happened and is happening to you is very relevant. Surely it is a complex subject and there are no easy answers. It seems to me a bit beastly to imagine that our Lord God dedicates himself to "sending" serious diseases to people to "get their attention." Surely this corresponds to an image of God that is not what Jesus has revealed to us. Another approach is to believe that the mystery of Evil (of which diseases are a part) is present in this world and we cannot escape it, and then, when we must live it and experience it, we can also in some way—with eyes of faith—see God's design. In any case, Jesus teaches us to give ourselves into the hands of the Father with total trust. And if we face our worldly lives in this way, we believe that we will also live with Him forever.

You will see, Magda, that my email today is not a marvel of clarity and precision. But there is, I think, a great passion for humanity. And I think that is what I have experienced with you and Marc during this year: a great passion for humanity, which means that very specific people always challenge our worldview and help us to grow in precisely what best defines us, to grow in humanity.

I am the one who is grateful to you for taking the parsley out of my ears* and accepting me as a special (spiritual) "resident" [as opposed to one of her medical residents].

I am still savoring the muffins.

> *"Taking parsley out of one's ears" must be explained. One day, in one of my conversations with Magda in Montserrat, she said something like this: "Let's see if we can all get God to take the parsley out of his ears, and he listens to us, and I get cured once and for all." My face showed that I didn't understand the metaphor, and Magda explained that this parsley idea was from the adventures of Asterix and Obelix.[18] In one of the battles against the Gauls, the Romans stuffed parsley in their ears so as not to hear the "songs" of the Welsh poet-singer Cacofonix, which were so horrible that they made the Romans so weak and disorganized that they fled in desperation. But of course it turns out that, with their ears full of parsley, the Romans had not heard their centurion's instructions at the time of the attack, and the whole thing ends comically, as usual. As Magda appreciated precision, one day she gave me a copy of the Asterix book with the parsley-in-the-ears adventure. She included this letter:

October 10, 2013

> As an editor, I like to find and read the original sources. I recommend pages 6 and 7, which are the basis of our conversation about parsley . . .

> I doubt that anyone has ever given a comic book to a prior, but this image of those who do not want to listen has been with me for many years, since I was the age for reading Asterix and Obelix.

> I know that this book is probably not appropriate or worthy of being put in the monastery library, but you may want to save it on your personal bookshelves.

> Thanks for everything you've taught me.

> Una abraçada

> Magda

Obviously, I keep this book and Magda's letter as one of the most beloved treasures on my shelves. For me, it reflects Magda's purity of heart, that childhood soul that she never lost and that made her so unique and so beloved.

Magda / October 6, 2013

Send me the phrase you mentioned from Fr. Duch so I can think about it . . .

Ignasi / October 6, 2013

The phrase is: "the symbols (examples of the intermediation humans cannot do without) mediate the presence of what is immediately absent."

*[Note: The original phrase, in Catalan, uses a play on words
that defies elegant translation: "aquells artefactes historico-
culturals que fan mediatament present allò que és immediata-
ment absent"—Lluís Duch, Joan-Carles Mèlich,* Ambigüitats
de l'Amor *(Barcelona: Abadia de Montserrat, 2003).]*

Magda / October 11, 2013

I am finishing the seventh hour of chemo infusion, which has
gone very well.

I got a call from a good friend of mine with whom I have
done a lot of research, Jaume Marrugat—who also came to
my birthday party. Today we had a "different" conversation,
about life, the meaning of everything, etc.

I commented on the phrase from Joan Oliver that I showed
you yesterday ("Sometimes I do not remember that I too must
die"), and he sent me this one from the Dalai Lama that I
find very appropriate: "There are only two days in the year
that nothing can be done. One is called Yesterday and the
other is called Tomorrow." I thought you would like it.

Ignasi / October 11, 2013

Indeed, very beautiful. In 1998-9 I met a Dr. Jaume Marrugat
at IMIM. He had an uncle who is a monk. With him we par-
ticipated in a study on oil and lipids. It must be the same
person.

It was fun. We had to consume a certain amount of oil in 24
hours for 15 days, and then we were analyzed. A monk who
liked to joke called the study *oleum bíbimus*, which means
literally: "We have drunk oil." *[And which is, in turn, a Catalan expression meaning: "We're done for!"]*

Magda / October 11, 2013

Luckily, you've lasted a long time!

Magda / October 28, 2013

A few weeks before this message, I had given Magda a copy of the *Rule of Saint Benedict* with glosses prepared by Father Abbot Cassià Just. Chapter V of the Rule deals with obedience.

> The first step of humility is unhesitating obedience, which comes naturally to those who cherish Christ above all. Because of the holy service they have professed, or because of dread of hell and for the glory of everlasting life, they carry out the superior's order as promptly as if the command came from God himself. The Lord says of men like this: *No sooner did he hear than he obeyed me* (Ps 17[18]:45); again, he tells teachers: *Whoever listens to you, listens to me* (Luke 10:16). Such people as these immediately put aside their own concerns, abandon their own will, and lay down whatever they have in hand, leaving it unfinished. (RB 5.1-8)

I am reading the Rule and I was very impressed by the issue of obedience . . . I hope that someday we will have time to talk about it.

In the part written by Abbot Cassià, there is a term that I don't know, "*novíssims*," and when I looked up the original quotation, it seemed to be related to death!?

At 11:00 tomorrow I have another PET scan, then at 4:00 a chemo session. I hope to get better news than with previous imaging tests. Please think of me especially tomorrow.

Thank you for the opportunity to talk about all these issues freely.

Ignasi / October 29, 2013

Every day I pray for you, but today you are especially present.

In theological terminology, the *novissimi [in Latin]* are the last realities of life: death, judgment (by God), hell, and glory. The *Catechism* speaks to this at line numbers 988–1065.[8]

Obedience is one of the great themes of the monastic tradition. Obviously, it is not synonymous with "group think." It has a lot to do with freedom and with the ability to listen (*oboedire*—to obey, in Latin—has the same etymological root as *obaudire*—to listen).

Magda / October 29, 2013

I will get my new PET results on November 4th when I visit the oncologist. Although I feel very well (except during the post-chemotherapy week), after the whole mess of images that I've had, every time I put myself into one of these machines, "I get scared."

Very interesting, your observation about obedience = freedom + listening. The first reading of the Rule actually gave me the feeling that I could never put up with the requirements it lays out, some of them a bit tough (even corporal punishment!).

I guess that's why I'm not a nun. . . Anyway, Griselda is also excited about her life as a nun (something we've talked about), and since I appreciate both of you a lot, I think maybe I've missed something, but I am very satisfied with my life as it is. To each his/her own!

I also pray for you (when I remember) ever since you told me that my prayers had an added value!

Magda / October 30, 2013

Good evening: I just saw you on *Telenoticies Nit (the evening TV news in Catalan]* explaining the Rule of Saint Benedict to a group of business leaders.

If you do another seminar like that, can I sign up or is it only for people from the business world? If not, we will have to do "private classes" so I can better understand its applicability to the 21st century. You already saw from the previous emails that I have many questions.

Congratulations on this initiative—surely it will be a success!

Ignasi / November 1, 2013

The next course on the Rule of Saint Benedict and leadership will be November 21-22. If that works for you, you can sign up, no problem; just say the word and you're invited.

Wednesday evening (it's always in the evening, when the qualified nurse has already left Montserrat!), I had to attend a lady who was in a bad state. Thank God it was nothing; but there were funny situations, which I cannot explain in writing.

Magda / November 1, 2013

I am free on November 21 and 22, and if it is not restricted to a closed group, I would like to be there. We will need to discuss the practical aspects (hotel, registration, level of prior knowledge, etc.). I'd like to see a syllabus of previous courses. Thank you very much for the invitation!

I did not go online for the Conventual Mass because it got too late. I spent the morning editing an urgent text, cooking sweet potatoes, and preparing quince . . . ("multitasking"). Not to say so myself, but everything tasted very good and the text has improved a lot. When I noticed it was already 11:45, I applied the saying of Saint Teresa (according to my mother), "God also walks among the pots and pans," and I stopped with just my morning psalms.

On Wednesday you had the classic evening or nighttime call; it seems that Murphy *[of Murphy's Law]* feels right at home at Montserrat. I can imagine some situations that are better not put into writing. In fact, doctors could write books that would be bestsellers.

Now I'll tell you about one that happened to me when I was just a resident and I had to leave the room to laugh until I could get serious again and continue.

When I was doing the hospital rotation for hemodynamics, in the afternoon before a catheterization we would visit the patients who were to have the procedure the next day. We examined them, paying special attention to the femoral pulses, and explained that we would put them under local anesthesia, puncture the artery without hurting them, inject contrast (under pressure, with some accompanying discomfort), apply digital compression for 20 minutes and then bandage them up, and then they would have to rest in bed for 24 hours.

Well, I went to see Mr. X (Spanish-speaking) and I said:

MH: Good afternoon. I am Dr. Heras and I am here to explain the catheterization *[in Spanish, cateterismo]*.

Mr. X: Thank you very much, Doctor, but I'm not interested.

MH: Excuse me, but I think you should be well informed and we need to talk about it.

Mr. X: I tell you with great conviction, I studied with the friars and I am very clear about this.

MH: Sorry, but I do not see the relationship between the friars and tomorrow's procedure.

Mr. X: You said that you came to explain the catechism to me and I repeat that it does not interest me.

I could barely tell him that he had confused the two words *[cateterismo* versus catecismo*]*—before running out of the room and laughing myself silly at the misunderstanding! You see that my capacity for proselytizing is nil!

Well, when I see you on the 16th you can tell me that story of yours, unless it's a professional secret.

Many greetings from Isil, with the trees all golden and already dropping their leaves. Glorious as always.

November 5, 2013

Dear friends and family:

You probably know that I had a "difficult" month of July because the drug I was taking as an oral medication stopped working for me. The tumor developed a resistance to it. Finally, and after many tests and premedication *[to ward off side effects]*, I began traditional chemotherapy on July 31st.

After four chemotherapy sessions with two drugs, last week's PET showed tumor stabilization; the oncologist told me this was good news because it looks like it will stay like this; in other words, it will become chronic and the objective for future treatment is to "keep it within bounds." On the other hand, the lab tests were back to normal.

Today I changed to a management chemotherapy that is administered in just 15 minutes; this is an important improvement because the previous doses kept me there for seven hours. In addition, it doesn't affect my veins and it appears that the side effects will be negligible. I'll know about that over the coming days, as individual responses vary.

I feel very good; I feel like doing things and I do them, including walks when we are in Isil. The other day I hiked up 400 meters within a short distance and wasn't short of breath—but I did it at my own pace. All the same, now I have to get back into physical shape because the four chemotherapy sessions left me with very little strength and quite tired.

Well, thanks for your interest and unconditional support in this "difficult" time, but it's "interesting" too, in a way, because of all that I have learned.

Una abraçada, Magda

Magda / November 5, 2013

I have sent you a copy of the update letter that I do for my friends and family. I find it a good way to keep them up to date, especially because they are grateful for news. Besides, their replies and the contact make me feel loved in a way that I would never have thought. I think we have talked about it before, but I find it to be a very rich experience.

The news from the oncologist was positive even though (in her words) it seems this tumor just won't go away; therefore, if it does not spread like it did last summer, that will be the best that can happen. In addition, I now find myself in good shape, although that's more mental and work-related than physical, but if the new chemo regimen means I won't be so wiped out, I will promptly begin a physiotherapy program before restarting tennis and swimming. Physical exercise is an important part of my life that I want to resume.

What I wanted to say at a more personal level is that yesterday evening's reading was Psalm 115-116 and it seemed tailor-made for the news that I got. I recited it with great pleasure because it expressed very well what I felt. There are also days that it seems to go the other way 'round, but according to Fr. Hilari, then one must adapt to focus on other people who may be suffering or enjoying situations different from ours. I find it harder but I make the effort.

Today I will only do half of my "homework" because between the chemo and the trip to Isil I could not say the Psalms in the morning. Now I will recite the afternoon ones because I have a cook: Marc has taken the week off to take care of me and is making dinner (an "Asian delight"). Oh! And I say the prayer of Simeon because it's short. The problem is that I usually do it in bed and sometimes life as a couple doesn't exactly facilitate one's concentration. This is why Saint Benedict was very clear that if you want to fully devote yourself to the life of "*l'ora et labora*" *[prayer and work]*, it is better to be alone. That's not my choice and so I do my best to combine "*l'ora*" with family and daily life.

I have written to Fr. Hilari and told him that you and I would work out the schedules for the visit with the Arzamendis on the 16th. I think we agreed to meet in the reception area after the Conventual Mass. We will visit the parts of the monastery you want to show them and part of the museum. I also understand that we will eat there; if that's not the case, tell me and

I'll make a reservation at Cisneros. If we have time before coming to see you, we will probably take the funicular so that they can see the landscape, since Begoña is seven months pregnant and hiking is not the best thing for her right now. They won't bring their son because our plan isn't designed for a two-year-old and what he wants and needs to do is run, play, and be able to take a good nap.

Forgive all the personal "news." I don't mean to be a bother but I like to share details with you.

Ignasi / November 6, 2013

I am grateful for the possibility of sharing some "more personal" things. As I always tell you, it's very good for me.

I'm glad about the oncologist's positive news. Perhaps Our Lord has removed the parsley from one ear, at least (forgive the irreverence, but you taught me the metaphor).

It's true what you said about the Psalms. There are days that they seem tailor-made for what we are living through. I think it is a privilege to have access to words to say and that express who we are and what we feel. In addition to expressing who we are, the words also help to create thoughts, and in some way to shape our being (but maybe I'm exaggerating). It is not by chance that the Gospel of Saint John begins with that expression: "In the beginning was the Word" (John 1:1). And the Word is Jesus, the Messiah.

As for the Arzamendi visit, I imagine it like this: we meet after Conventual Mass in the reception area. I have to welcome a pilgrimage group on behalf of Father Abbot, who will be away. I will leave you with Fr. Hilari, who can show you the library and other rooms of the monastery.

I will join the group as soon as I finish my duties. We'll eat at the hostelry and after lunch go to the museum (depending on how Fr. Hilari is feeling, he can accompany us or not). All this, with the changes and adaptations that are best made on the fly.

I have registered you for the course on the Rule of Saint Benedict and values in leadership, on November 21 and 22. I'll give you more details when we see each other.

Magda / November 30, 2013

Tomorrow I will stop by after the Conventual Mass to see you for a while.

One thing is the distribution of the Psalms because as you gave them to me there were many that I did not read. I made this grid in Excel, if you want to look at it.

Let's discuss it tomorrow!

> Magda was a very good student. She took things very seriously. She ended up knowing more than the "teacher." An example is the distribution of all the Psalms that she herself designed in order to be able to pray them all.

	W1 Sun	W1 Mon	W1 Tue	W1 Wed	W1 Thu	W1 Fri	W1 Sat
Wake-up	95, 3, 67	95, 3, 67	95, 3, 67	95, 3, 67	95, 3, 67	95, 3, 67	95, 3, 67
Morning	51, 118, 63	5, 36	43, 57	64, 65	88, 90	76, 92	143
Vespers	110-113	114-116, 128	130-133	135-138	139-141	142, 144, 145	145-147
Night	3, 91, 134	3, 91, 134	3, 91, 134	3, 91, 134	3, 91, 134	3, 91, 134	3, 91, 134

	W2 Sun	W2 Mon	W2 Tue	W2 Wed	W2 Thu	W2 Fri	W2 Sat
Wake-up	1, 2, 6	1, 2, 6	1, 2, 6	1, 2, 6	1, 2, 6	1, 2, 6	1, 2, 6
Morning	9, 10, 11	16, 17	19-21	25-27	31-33	38-40	
Vespers	12-15	18	22-24	28-30	34, 35, 37	41, 44(II)	
Night	4, 7, 8	4, 7, 8	4, 7, 8	4, 7, 8	4, 7, 8	4, 7, 8	4, 7, 8
	W3 Sun	W3 Mon	W3 Tue	W3 Wed	W3 Thu	W3 Fri	W3 Sat
Wake-up	50, 52, 53	50, 52, 53	50, 52, 53	50, 52, 53	50, 52, 53	50, 52, 53	50, 52, 53
Morning	58, 59, 60	68, 69	73, 74	78	81, 82, 83	87, 93	94, 96, 97
Vespers	61, 62, 66	70-72	75, 77	79, 80	84-86	89	98-100
Night	54-56	54-56	54-56	54-56	54-56	54-56	54-56
	W4 Sun	W4 Mon	W4 Tue	W4 Wed	W4 Thu	W4 Fri	W4 Sat
Wake-up	101-103	101-103	101-103	101-103	101-103	101-103	101-103
Morning	104	106	119	119	123, 124	127, 128	149
Vespers	105	107	119	120-122	125, 126	148	150
Night	108, 109	108, 109	108, 109	108, 109	108, 109	108, 109	108, 109

Magda / December 3, 2013

In Madrid it has been even colder than at Montserrat, and today I was able to go to the gym and pool because my myalgia went away. I am celebrating with a good black tea and chocolate, waiting for Marc—who has already arrived in Madrid *[from an international trip]*. I will find some good psalms for the evening . . . the Abbess* allows it.

*In one of our conversations, and I don't quite remember how, the metaphor of the Mother Abbess came about. This was normal, given the importance of the figure of the Abbot in the Rule of Saint Benedict and in monastic life. The "game" was very innocent: just as I have an Abbot whom I must obey, Magda had her Abbess (which after all was her own good heart) to whom, in turn, she had to give obedience. The game lasted until the day before Magda's death. Already confined to her bed, in a moment of clarity she said: "Now I cannot pray psalms; I am very weak." I answered, with great emotion, "The Mother Abbess will understand perfectly."

Magda / December 16, 2013

From December 9th to 16th, I went to the Benedictine Abbey in Montecassino, Italy, to lead spiritual exercises in the community. Then I spent a couple of days in Rome. Before leaving, I had given Magda and Marc two tickets for a Christmas concert at the Sagrada Família. [Note: This is the famously "unfinished" modernist cathedral by architect Antoni Gaudí, now nearly finished.]

I don't know if you have access to email in Rome, but if not you will find this one (with a few hundred more!) when you arrive at Montserrat.

Yesterday we went to the concert in Sagrada Família; I attach the program for you. The choir and musicians were very good, but the height of the church eats up the sound, although the reverberation is really not as much as one might expect from seeing the structure.

I really liked that they sang the Christmas carols arranged by Guinovart because we had just been looking for this recording to give to the journal's collaborators but it turned out that it's already out of print. In the end, I bought carols sung by the *Escolania*, so now I'm advertising them "in Spain" [*i.e., outside of Catalonia*].

By the way, this week on Channel 33 I saw an interview with Fr. Lluís Duch, the "intermediation" guy, and I was impressed by his speaking and reasoning. Today I went to hear Fr. Hilari at the Bar Association talking about Manuel Carrasco i Formiguera [*Catalan lawyer and Christian Democrat, 1890-1938; executed in Burgos by Franco's army in the Spanish Civil War*]. He was brilliant, but he made me worry because, obviously, he did not follow my advice to speak slowly. He raced to say everything in 40 minutes and didn't stop even to take a sip of water! And the best thing was that he had no dyspnea. When he finished, I went to tell him that I saw he was in fine form, and he laughed.

The more I know, the more intrigued I am to know how the Rule of Saint Benedict can accommodate all these "brains" under the same roof for life, without harming day-to-day relationships.

By the way, Father Abbot told me that you are coming back tomorrow and he leaves for Rome and Montecassino the next day . . . He said that you had gone to prepare the soil. He was very kind and told me that he knew my father.

Today I had the umpteenth lab tests and saw the oncologist. Everything is stable and the best thing is that I remain in full physical and psychological form, although I have to admit that I increasingly get nervous when I turn on the computer to look at test results or images.

Tomorrow they will give me the maintenance chemo. The doctor has explained that the myalgia I have, and likely will continue to have, is one of the side effects of Premetexed . . . this has taken a weight off me, and ended the temptation to turn it over and over in my head more than necessary. As we have discussed several times, the challenge of the disease is more mental than physical and that does not change over time, although fortunately I have found many tools to channel my brain when it overflows. You have been an active collaborator, and thanks again for that.

I hope that your work in Montecassino was pleasant and effective, and above all that you enjoyed your time in Rome and speaking Italian.

Ciao and until Saturday (a sample of my "lamentable" Italian skills).

Ignasi / December 17, 2013

Ciao dottoressa [Hello, Madame Doctor]: Thanks to modern technology, I've been able to read your email. I'm really glad about the news you shared.

I'll tell you later about Montecassino.

In Rome, I arrived Saturday afternoon and leave at midday today *[Tuesday]*. This city has stolen my heart. I have walked a lot (very healthy from a cardiovascular point of view, right?), and I have been immersed in this simultaneously local and cosmopolitan atmosphere. *Na meraviglia [a marvel]*, as the Romans say.

Magda / December 17, 2013

Physical exercise is very beneficial for cardiovascular health but also for mental well-being, although that is scientifically more difficult to evaluate! Therefore, these days you are accumulating a double dose of good health. I hope to see you rejuvenated this Saturday!

I have been in Rome four times, very little, but I was impressed by the Roman Forum and the Villa Borghese (especially the sculptures). The Trastevere street life is also interesting, to take in this more local and less cosmopolitan aspect. We'll talk soon.

They've just given me the medication and tomorrow and Thursday I'll be back in Madrid again; it's a good time to go there because they invariably want to talk about the referendum![19]

Magda / December 27, 2013

Good morning. Today I got up early because I have a PET scan (aiyiyi! . . .) and I followed along during Lauds using the Book of Hours, but unsuccessfully because I thought it was the Feast of Saint John* (??). Finally I ended with the psalms approved by my Abbess . . . . Have a good day! . . . and "pray" for me.[20]

    *It was John the Baptist, not the Apostle.

Ignasi / December 27, 2013

Do what the Mother Abbess says, no problem! I pray for you.

Magda / December 29, 2013

    To celebrate their 37th wedding anniversary, Magda and Marc spent a couple of days at Montserrat.

We really enjoyed our several visits with you yesterday, especially in the evening, although Marc made us all go to sleep "early" (maybe you also appreciated that). Please thank your prior for being such an understanding and generous guy! *[Note: Ignasi IS, of course, the prior.]*

Today I left Mass feeling frustrated. The reading of the letter from Saint Paul regarding the submission of the wife to her husband is so out of date that—even though I understand it was written maaaaaaany years ago—it hurts the ears and the heart to keep hearing it . . . Can't you do something to adapt these texts to current sensibilities? Precisely today, the day we were married 37 years ago, I think that our partnership's success has been our ongoing pact to support each other, simultaneously, where family and professional activities were concerned, without either of us having to renounce an opportunity to do something interesting. In many couples that don't last, the origin of the problem is precisely the domination of one over the other. Doesn't it seem deeply unfair that 50% of the population has to be subjected to the other sex that for "unknown" reasons is the stronger sex? I would like to know how the women priests* of the Anglican church have resolved this issue.

You see that I am belligerent on this point, but it reminds me of that verse of a Psalm that says the children of Babylon must be smashed against the rocks. One day you told me that some pope had said that due to respect for current sensibilities this verse should be removed. I propose that this phrase of Saint Paul's also be revised . . . but I do not know anybody I should talk to other than your always attentive and patient ears.

*[*Note: Magda used the term women "ministers."]*

Magda / January 1, 2014

Marc and I want to share with you our joy at having started another new year together, which we hope will bring us health and the possibility to enjoy more visits with you.

This afternoon we're going to Isil until the 5th.

Greetings from us to the monks we know.

Ignasi / January 1, 2014

Thank you very much, Magda. I also wish the same. I have a few pending assignments from you, and they're not easy ones. I hope to respond in the next few days. Isil must be as beautiful in winter as in summer!

Magda / January 1, 2014

If you prefer, let's talk; maybe that would be better, instead of written monologues. I can come on Friday the 10th, morning or afternoon.

Isil is a wonder when there is snow. I will try to ski. Yesterday I was able to play tennis with the trainer for an hour (at "tumor pace"). You cannot imagine the feelings of well-being and joy that I get from these returns to "normality." I think I was saying phrases from the Lord's Prayer between swings of the racquet because I was feeling so happy and grateful!

Winter in Isil

Magda / January 5, 2014

Isil this morning, after the snowfall of yesterday evening, is beautiful! Today we followed the Conventual over the Internet. THANKS for providing the song title and composer in your voice-over.

On Friday afternoon we go back to Isil for the weekend. If you want to come, you are invited!

Ignasi / January 5, 2014

Thank you very much, Magda, but next weekend I am also "on call" because Father Abbot will be away. *Una abraçada*

Magda / January 5, 2014

Too bad that Saint Benedict did not foresee the possibility of "selling" your on-call duty as we do in hospitals. I'll see you next Friday.

Ignasi / January 5, 2014

This reminds me of a joke from Forges in JANO magazine *[a Spanish "medicine and humanities" journal]*. Two residents are negotiating about their on-call shift (the Barça *[Barcelona soccer team]* was having a really bad year in the Spanish League): R#1 says, "If you take my shift on Saturday, I'll shout fervently, 'Long live the Barça.' " R#2 replies: "Three times, and in the cafeteria." R#1: "Deal."

January 9, 2014

Dear family and friends:

Almost 16 months after the diagnosis, I'm still alive and kickin', as our great-grandmother used to say, and you know that I'm very happy to be here and glad that you let me share this life experience with you. It helps me so much.

Today I passed another ITV and now I have the PET results from December 27th. In short, the disease is stable and I will continue, for now, with the same medication (intravenous chemotherapy every three weeks, lasting just 10 minutes!).

As you know, I tolerate this treatment much better than the previous longer sessions, and it has the added benefit of giving me a "new look" because instead of losing my hair, it's getting curly and it looks like I got a permanent. At least, it's all natural (except the color, as some of you have noticed). There has to be some advantage in all this, no?

I've made a deal with my oncologist that she will let me go back to work because clinically I am doing really well. I have gone back to exercising, swimming, a little tennis, and a few hikes that went pretty well. All of this has helped me recover the physical and moral strength I had lost.

I miss having contact with patients and medical residents, which are the best jobs I've ever had. I want to start working half-time to see how it goes. Frankly, since I feel well, I'm starting to get a little cabin fever from staying home. Now I've gotten used to not thinking about the future beyond tomorrow because I think that it's better for my mental health that way . . . and besides, the future keeps arriving by the grace of God, although sometimes with some unexpected surprises.

So, celebrate this good news with us and, if you want, I'll be in touch if there is any more news.

Thank you for keeping me company. I wish you good health for the new year, 2014.

Magda / January 10, 2014

Instructions for making a good herbal infusion:

1 teaspoon of herbs per cup (the spoon is in the teapot; it also serves as a clamp to close the bag) + 200 cc of boiling water per cup.

Let it steep for the range of time recommended on the package (I always prefer the shorter time; otherwise I find them too strong, but it depends on individual taste).

I included a very aromatic Rooibos, from a South African plant that has no theine *[a stimulant similar to caffeine]*, which is ideal in the evening because it won't keep you awake.

Let me know if the selection is to your liking.

And thank you for the nice visit we shared.

Ignasi / January 10, 2014

Thanks to you, and also for the instructions. I had no idea what to do with that really strong clip with the spoon on its tip. I probably would have put it in the kettle!

The best thing was the "Palace Pantry" box of muffins. On Google, your name comes up before "Magdalenas Heras-Bareche"!

[Note: The Heras-Bareche company manufactures "magdalenas" (muffins) in Spain's Huesca province; Ignasi suggests Magda Heras is more famous than the Heras-Bareche factory brand.]

Magda / January 10, 2014

As my grandmother would say, "You can stir a lot of that into the pot," meaning "that's irrelevant." The best thing is to make family and friends happy with something as insignificant as muffins. Enjoy them!

Magda / January 18, 2014

Taking advantage of your generous offer "to edit and strengthen" my letter to the bishop responsible for "biblical terminology," I attach what I have written so that you can make any comments you consider appropriate (total freedom!). I read it to Marc and, with an ironic smile, he said that it's time for me to go back to my job. But I want to send the letter. I think genetics is "taking over" because this reaction is typical of my father!

I have started the process of getting approval to return to work and I am waiting for Social Security to approve it. I am also talking with the hospital about working half-days. I do not want to go from nothing to everything at once! I continue my "normal" life (editorial job and the online master's degree), physical exercise, walking . . . and I am "delighted with life" *[encantada de la vida]* (never before so well said!).

I also attach a link to the text that was prepared about my father when he was named Terrassa's Person of the Year. As you'll see, it is based on his CV that I sent you previously.

By the way, at the Municipal Plenary at the end of January, my father will be awarded the city's Gold Medal, and the mayor and the councilor for culture will go to visit him on January 27th to announce it to him in person. That's a nice gesture because in other cases the mayor does it by telephone, but given my father's age, they decided to make a home visit.

How are you? And "my patients"?

January 18, 2014

Magda's letter to the Bishop of La Seu d'Urgell, as revised

Monsignor Joan-Enric Vives Sicilia,
    I address you, the president of the Commission on Liturgy of the Tarragona Episcopal Conference, and therefore also the Commission of Liturgical Versions, to

send a comment on the reading of the Letter from Saint Paul to the Colossians 3:18-20 during the Mass of the Feast of the Holy Family, on December 29th.

As you know, the text of the Lectionary says: "Women, be submissive to your husbands." Hearing this phrase, as read and with no interpretation, creates discomfort in present times.

I am aware that the text was written in a very different social context from how we live today. In addition, I know the difficulty of translating a text originally written in other languages (Hebrew, Greek, Latin) and keeping "the spirit" of the writer. However, I do believe that the expression "submissive to your husband" should be revised, given all that the word "submission" entails for women. In fact, synonyms for this concept include "subjugation, subjection, subordination, capitulation, compliance," among others.

I do not think that the idea of the current family can be based on the husband's dominion over the wife; on the contrary, it must be the result of a relationship of free choice, consensus, and active participation on both sides.

That is why, hearing these words "cold," they give me a sense of frustration because it seems we are not capable of finding words that can actively engage women of the 21st century in the concept of the Christian couple.

As a personal note I would add that, on December 29th, my husband and I celebrated our 37th wedding anniversary, and maybe that is why I found the word "submissive" an even more unfortunate word choice. One of our successes as a couple has been a relationship of equals that has allowed us to develop our family life and also to make it compatible with our respective professions, without either one of us having to submit to the other.

Share, collaborate, listen, help, etc. . . . these would be much more just and would reflect the current reality for couples who succeed!

I am at your disposal for any clarification that might be necessary.

Many thanks for your attention. Receive a cordial greeting from

Magda Heras

Magda / January 20, 2014

Thank you so much, Ignasi, for adding details in the letter. Today I sent it, and I hope they'll answer me.*

I read it to my mother, who asked me for a copy to share with a friend of hers. She told me that the Teams of Our Lady, of which they are members, once sent a letter to the Vatican when Paul VI was pope, asking for a review of Church doctrine on contraception and they are still waiting for somebody to answer them!

Yesterday was my father's saint's day and I organized a dinner at our house to celebrate with the whole family. There were 31 of us, and my brother Lluís and some of the brothers-in-law made a "mega-paella" that was really good.

Today I bought the book by Ravasi** and also *Get Married and Be Submissive****; once I got started on the subject, I've already given it a polyhedral twist! When I've finished the book, I will pass it on to you before my daughter thinks I've lost my mind.

Thanks again for your Benedictine patience.

*Bishop Joan Enric Vives answered Magda's letter with a handwritten note dated February 27, 2014 (reproduced below).

La Seu, II.27.14

Benvolguda [Dear + feminine ending]

Thank you for your letter of January 18, and most of all congratulations for 37 years as a married couple. I give thanks to God for your love, as you both do!

And about Saint Paul . . . as difficult as it may be, it is written that way. It is necessary to contextualize all of the readings from the Old (maybe more so) and New Testaments. But when we understand them well, they are the path to God.

Let's see if we can find a more appropriate word than "submission," which I also see as not very appropriate.

Very cordially,

+ Joan E. Vives

**This book by Cardinal Gianfranco Ravasi, *The Encounter: Discovering God through prayer.* [In Catalan: *La Trobada. Retrobar-se en la pregària* (Barcelona, Editorial Claret, 2013)], contains the exercises he prepared for Pope Benedict XVI in February 2013, based on texts from the Psalms. Ravasi is a renowned specialist on the book of Psalms.

***This book, by the Italian journalist Costanza Miriano, published by the Diocese of Granada [in Spanish, *Cásate y sé sumisa* (Granada, Editorial Nuevo Inicio, 2013)], caused a resounding controversy that resulted in complaints to the public prosecutor—which is easy to imagine just from the title. After reading it, Magda gave it to me somewhat secretively, because it was not "politically correct" to be interested in this book. That Magda talked to me about it was, for me, an example of her free spirit and her sense of humor.

Magda / January 22, 2014

Got any suggestions to make Psalm 119 "less arid"? Although I have divided it into three parts, I find it "boring, for being so repetitive." I will appreciate suggestions (if there are any!).

Ignasi / January 22, 2014

The easiest thing is to do it in small pieces, as small as you want, and distribute them over time as you like. It's like chocolates: a whole box at once is undigestible, but one every now and then . . . on the other hand, they do all taste a lot alike.

February 1, 2014

Excerpt from a letter to close friends in Terrassa

Dear Salvador and Maria,

I'll bring you up to date on the last few hours since we saw each other on Wednesday. As you know, I returned from our trip to Florence with something I thought was the flu. That week I had a fever that went away with acetaminophen. Thursday afternoon (when I hadn't had a fever for 24 hours) we went to Isil because we had arranged to meet friends there. When we got as far as Llavorsí, I started to shiver with cold. It was the fastest round-trip we've ever made. After having a fever all night (38.5° *[101°F]*), we went to Hospital Clínic at 8:00 a.m.

The lab tests ruled out the flu (I'd had a flu shot) and suggested a bacterial infection, probably respiratory, but without a cough and with a chest X-ray that looked pretty darned good (I imagined it LOTS worse).

They gave me an intravenous antibiotic and new oral antibiotics, and Monday I have a checkup and we'll see about the results. I, good little patient that I am, feel very well, with only minor complaints, and this is a diagnostic challenge for my hospital colleagues (that always happens—doctors never have normal diseases).

Well, now you're up to date on my "sorry state." (Hey, that rhymes!)

Good health! (because all other good things will follow on their own.)

Magda / February 2, 2014

Thank you for the afternoon. We did not stay for Vespers because I felt like I was getting a fever. I'm now at *38° [100.4° F]*. Let's see if tomorrow the lab analysis gives me good news.

Ignasi / February 2, 2014

Amen.

Magda / February 4, 2014

Some Americans who want to spend Easter in Catalunya have asked me if the *Escolania* will be there Easter Sunday or will be away for the holiday. They would like to come to Mass at Montserrat, but they want to know if there will be music "*in excelsis.*"

Thank you for the writings of Fr. Ribera, so full of sanity and inclusiveness.

These were notes written by Fr. Ramon Ribera, monk and Bible scholar, for homilies about the phrase "women, submit yourselves to your husbands" from Col 3:18 that had moved Magda to write to Bishop Vives.

One day you'll have to tell me if, when you become monks, you also drink a "potion" that makes you all be so understanding, or is it that the re-reading of the Rule works wonders . . . light-years from "our Costanza," author of "the book."

Two considerations *[about "the book"]* that I did not mention: Reading it and having raised a family, I had the sense that this woman is an "arrogant superwoman," and the second and most important is that I had the feeling I was reading about how to organize a single-parent family, where the fathers just chime in on the tasks she considers to be properly theirs.

I'm managing, with a slight fever in the evenings but it's less every day, I hope that Thursday's lab tests will continue to show improvement.

I liked the text from Fr. Hilari* very much, and I'm sure it helped me to refocus my prayers with the psalms that I sometimes read too routinely. I'll keep the text for you until I see you. I thank you for your friendship and prayers for me as well as the prayers of the other monks who know me.

*"El temps del lector" [The Reader's Turn], written by Fr. Hilari Raguer about his fellow disciple and friend Josep M. Castellet, in which he offers the thesis that when a writer has published a work, it ceases to be his, in a sense, because each reader can understand it in a very personal way, and then he applies this to the way in which the monks recite the Psalms.

Ignasi / February 4, 2014

The students *[escolans]* are in Montserrat until Conventual Mass on Easter. Once the Mass is over and Virolai has been sung, they go off on vacation with their families all Easter week. If your American friends come to Montserrat for the Easter Sunday Conventual Mass (at 11:00 a.m., as usual) they can still hear the *Escolania*.

It is worth saying that Fr. Ramon Ribera is a "specialist" in what you call "this compassionate nature thing." Perhaps because he knows the biblical texts in the original languages, and therefore he can better delve into their deep meaning and the elements that have been added by cultures and the passage of time, not to mention by new translations.

Oh, by the way, I am not aware that they give us any "potion" when we become monks, at least not that I know of. Unless the "potion" is monastic life in and of itself: *ora* (pray), *et lege* (and read), *et labora* (and work) *in communitate* (in community), which means that whatever makes you most irritable with a brother in the community is probably something you also do, and makes another person crazy, and thus, on the basis of walking our path together, what happens to us is like the pebbles in the river that, by colliding with each other, become rounder and smooth off their rough edges.

About "the book," we have to talk in person. I have not gotten past the first pages, but at first glance I completely agree with what you say. It is full of clichés that sometimes even make you tired because they are such well-worn topics. In addition, the style seems very journalistic, or more like a script for a television (or YouTube) monologue than a book. She seems to try for a frenetic pace that wears me out. Now, that being said, I can imagine a true Roman "*mamma*" saying a good part of the things that the book says, but in Italian and gesturing properly, and I assure you it would be much more fun.

Perhaps the main problem with the book is that they have translated it into Spanish and, of course, everything is so "hard-hitting" (*verdades como puños. . . que atontan como puñetazos*) [*quoted in Spanish; in English, "truths like fists . . . that punch you silly"*] and at the first "punch" you're already "groggy." On the other hand, in Italian you can go through pages and pages and the same reference to Saint Paul can go almost unnoticed. Another thing is that there are some interesting ideas about the human person and about marriage itself, but these are left hanging in the middle of the trumpeting and theatricality of the narrator. *Insomma [In conclusion . . .]*

I hope the slight fever finally goes away and you can go back to work soon.

Una abraçada and greetings to Marc (I forgot to tell him that I find the English names of some carpal bones*—which are actually in Latin—fantastic!)

> *A few days earlier I had read the scientific articles that Magda, Marc, and Anna gave me in September 2013 on the occasion of XXV years of monastic profession.

Magda / February 5, 2014

Thank you for the reply. We will get together for tea and finish talking about the *mammas* of Rome. I share with you the feeling of exhaustion that you get after a few moments of reading "the book."

Very interesting, the concept of "river pebbles" that get polished. They certainly give you a way of being that is unmistakable!

I take this opportunity to ask about today's Vespers, which I followed online. I picked up the liturgical *Dietari [a book published annually by the monastery, which includes the liturgical calendar that regulates the community's prayer]* and I saw that today is Saint Agatha, virgin and martyr. Questions:

1.- What do the abbreviations mean . . . Sol (solemnity?) Mem, Feast (what does it mean?). I understand that when there is one of these abbreviations it means some change from the texts in the Book of Hours.

Some time earlier I had given Magda a simple volume of the Liturgy of the Hours with the prayers for Lauds, Vespers, and Compline each day. [In the US, this is called the Ordo or Liturgical Guide.]

2.- What do the numbers mean (these are for today): 2 S 24, 2-9 17 / Mc 6, 1-6. Unless I misunderstood, you read from Saint Peter.

3.- You always sing the entrance hymn in Latin (some special reason?). Today did you use the common prayer for the martyrs? or the virgins? (What prevails in these cases of duplication?)

4.- I was very happy because I could at least follow the Psalms but I have not been able to relate them to the numbers in point #2.

5.- Is the Magnificat in Latin for some reason?

Well, I must seem to you like a pesky fly that does not stop asking you things. Anyway, it was you who gave me the Book of Hours, and so to me it is almost a matter of honor to understand how you monks use it. Otherwise following along with Vespers on the Internet turns into a "drama" while I try not to get lost. Maybe, as Marc says, what I need to do is go back to work!

Marc is very proud that you liked the names of the bones and the tendons so much and that his field interests you. They are a great part of his life. . . as far as I know, the only "rival" that I have.

I have not had any more fever. Today I received the discharge to go back to work but tomorrow I have another round of tests, and if all goes well, new chemo. In agreement with my "boss," I will not go back until February 17th when I have recovered more.

Ignasi / February 6, 2014

I am very glad that you no longer have a fever and that you can predict the day you will return to work.

Don't worry about your questions; I have a lot of fun answering them. Every time it's like a small challenge. Besides, I've always liked to "explain" things so that others can understand them. I would be able to explain an interventricular communication secondary to an infarction of the inferior wall to a shepherd from the Pyrenees, but it would be even more exciting for me to explain the Na-K cell membrane pump to him.

I will, therefore, answer your questions, and with the same numbering:

1. Sol = solemnity; Festa = feast day; Mem = memorial *[commemoration]*. From the liturgical point of view, the days are not all the same. They can be classified into four categories, from minor to major importance: *fèria* (=weekdays); *memòria* = weekdays on which a saint is especially commemorated; *festa* = weekdays (or sometimes Sundays) on which a special *festa [feast day]* is celebrated (pardon the redundancy), such as February 2nd = the Presentation of our Lord in the Temple,

also known as Candlemas; and finally *solemnitat* = the great "solemn" liturgical celebrations of the year such as Christmas, Easter, Pentecost, the great solemnities of the Virgin Mary, etc. . . .

2. The "numbers," as you say, are the biblical references for the readings of the Mass. In this way we monks (the one who has to prepare the homily for a given day, for example, or who has to read) know in advance what readings there will be at Mass that day. However, the daily "brief reading" for Lauds and Vespers does not appear in the liturgical *Dietari [they are printed periodically by each monastery as a separate list of readings]*.

3. The hymn in Latin at the beginning is what little remains of when everything was done in Latin and Gregorian. It must be said that the hymns that have been done in Catalan aren't the best, except for those by two monks (words by Fr. Hildebrand Miret and music by Fr. Ireneu Segarra) and sometimes we sing them at matins for some solemnities. In "the order" of the saints, martyrs go before virgins, because martyrdom implies "literally" giving up one's life.

4. The answer is obvious, because they are totally unrelated, except that in both cases they are biblical texts. Thinking of your struggles to follow the Liturgy of the Hours, I am reminded of what happens to me when I read one of your "erudite" articles and on the fourth page I find an abbreviation something like AVKASHJGH that only the four of you who use it every day (or every other day, ha ha) know what it means, and I have to go back to the beginning of the article until I find the first time it appears and that is where I see what it means.

5. We sing the Magnificat in Latin and Gregorian (what a marvel!) only on the few days when the antiphon is also in Latin and Gregorian (but not always; we are the kings of

complication: that is, there are days when we sing the antiphon in Latin and the Magnificat in Catalan and others when we sing all in Latin). The reason was not to lose some antiphons in Latin and Gregorian that are especially well-known or meaningful for the monks.

I think that all this is the result of a liturgical reform that "simplified" many things (ha, ha, ha). Before the *[Second Vatican]* Council, praying from the Liturgy of Hours (or the Breviary, as they called it then) would have been even more "chiripitiflautical."[21]

Marc (writing for Magda) / February 23, 2014

Today it is not Magda bringing you news. It's me, Marc. She will do it when she can. We hope it will be soon.

For the past month, Magda has had sporadic episodes of fever. The fever was accompanied by erratic muscular pains and tiredness, which first made us think it could be flu, and later on maybe pneumonia. The test results three weeks ago seemed to suggest this last option, so they prescribed antibiotics. The fever disappeared, and we calmed down. Unfortunately, it's back. Yesterday, in the earliest hours of Saturday morning, it reached 39.5° *[103.1° F]*, which forced us to take her to Hospital Clínic.

The first test results continue to indicate a bacterial infection, but for now they have not found the source. Neither the chest X-ray nor abdominal ultrasound have clarified anything. More imaging tests (echocardiography, thoraco-abdominal CAT scan with contrast . . .) are pending. The goal is to find where the bacteria come from, which from time to time circulate in her blood and cause her these high fever peaks. When they figure it out, they can choose a definitive treatment.

Luckily, the tumor is still well under control, the fever responds well to medication, and except for the fever spikes, she feels well, has an appetite, and wants to do things. They have told us that the antibiotics will be administered intravenously until the infection is under control; that is, a few days. She is in room 9 of the "post-coronary" unit (1st stairwell, 6th floor). In principle, no one has told her that she cannot receive visits or phone calls. Even so, I think it's better that, until she has no fever, she be able to rest.

Now it's six o'clock Sunday morning, and I'm just about to leave for the airport to pick up Anna when she arrives from San Francisco, where she gave a research presentation in her specialty to an international conference. She does not yet know that her mother is in the hospital because she was already on a plane when Magda got the fever. As soon as she arrives, we will go to Hospital Clínic to see Magda.

I've written this so you know what the situation is at our house. I sincerely believe that everything will be fine, and that soon she herself will be able to write one of her "epistles."

Magda / February 23, 2014

I hope to visit you next Saturday or Sunday. For any question you can call me. I am admitted to "my hospital," with nurses who have been my colleagues for many years.

I'm having fever spikes and they've got me on Tazocel (i.v. antibiotic). For now, normal abdominal echo, echocardiogram, and chest X-rays. Pending lab cultures and a talk with the oncologist. I think that I "caught" this bacterium in Florence and because it must speak Italian it doesn't "get" what we try to tell it. Good night!

Ignasi / February 23, 2014

Try saying: "*xxx'xx xxxx, xxxxxxx xx xxxxx,*" which is a pretty nasty insult—although you could use a more elegant formula, like: "Sarebbe così gentile di andarsene da un'altra parte, per carità?" [*Would you be so kind as to go away, please?*]

Magda / February 23, 2014

I will speak to it now in Italian using the more polite formula. We must never lose our manners!

Ignasi / February 23, 2014

Thank you. Even in your present situation you teach me things.

Magda / February 27, 2014

PET results: Pulmonary and bone lesions are stable, but the liver has more of them. Tomorrow a liver biopsy to see if this tumor is a new mutant and they can give me a drug for it that they have at Vall d'Hebron (which seems very effective). I have less fever but we still don't know where it comes from. Will you think it strange if I tell you that I am a bit tired and disappointed?

C'mon, say something, whether it makes me laugh or not.

Ignasi / February 27, 2014

I don't find it strange, no. Sometimes it is difficult to find words. I suppose the psalmists also must have felt helpless sometimes, and perhaps they expressed only a moan, or a shout, or silence before God.

Magda / February 27, 2014

The only psalms that are working for me are #6 and #13 and I am repeating them. I think that thousands of years ago the anguish in the face of disease was identical to that of the 21st century.

Magda / February 28, 2014

Today was a better day, after "the hard drive" had processed the news that it did not want to receive. Now comes the third round and I will change chemo again. The liver biopsy went very well; I had an anesthetist who babied me!

Tomorrow I go home. If I can, we would come to Conventual Mass and also see our patients. In any case, can I ask you to reserve seats? I could not handle standing-room. If you never "take reservations," we'll come another day.

Thank you for your prayers. I do what I can, but basically I ask the *Moreneta*[22] to make me strong, mixed with the occasional Lord's Prayer. My Abbess is compassionate and doesn't "push me."

Ignasi / February 28, 2014

Thanks, Magda. I was in the Basilica recording Lenten responsorial psalms for our website. No problem booking seats. Your Abbess is a holy woman, who wants not submission but free will. Good night!

Magda / March 3, 2014

Yesterday evening 38.8° *[101.84°]*!! I was about to make a will. I'm sure our visit with you had nothing to do with it, quite the opposite. You said that from Wednesday to Saturday you will have spiritual exercises. If I need you, can I send WhatsApps or phone you?

Marc will be in Dubai those same days. Thanks for everything.

Ignasi / March 3, 2014

"Mannagia 'a miseria! sta febbre!" *[Goshdarn that miserable fever!]*

Magda / March 5, 2014

Summary of Hospital Clínic visit. A little anemia, waiting to see if last week's cultures are definitively negative. High inflammatory markers. Increasingly, it seems clearer that all this is due to progression of the disease. Monday I have an appointment and then I will start the new chemotherapy. Meanwhile, couch, books, and LOTSSsssaaa patience.

Ignasi / March 5, 2014

Ciao, dottoressa. Thanks for the information. I am with you!

Magda / March 5, 2014

I wanted to ask you if you have any special instructions for me for Lent. But with what I have, I think that will be enough. Thanks for keeping me company.

Ignasi / March 5, 2014

Indeed. You have more than enough. Saint Benedict recommends reading a book of the Bible for Lent. I recommend the gospels. There are four books, but they are not long. *Una abraçada!*

Magda / March 9, 2014

Everything is going very well. I still have no fever. We had lunch with friends, who have just left. I have begun reading the Gospel of Matthew; I'll read one after the other. Tomorrow I will explain the new treatment program.

Magda / March 10, 2014

They did not find the mutation they were looking for. Now it's chemotherapy (1h every 3 weeks) and an oral inhibitor, similar to what I took initially.

Side effects: tiredness, diarrhea, mouth sores, hair loss.

I will go to have a wig made, and it is the "perfect" time to change my look. What would you all prefer? blonde? red-head? salt-and-pepper? or it can also be my normal color. Knowing me, surely that is the one I will choose!

I begin chemotherapy tomorrow at 5:00 p.m. Let's see if they can give it a good whack and make it leave me alone for another good chunk of time.

Later I will send you an email, perhaps with less banal reflections.

Ignasi / March 10, 2014

1st reaction: "mannagia 'a miseria!" *[Goshdarnit!]*

2nd reaction: Even in this situation you keep your humor (I vote for red hair) and you "keep it together." (Hats off to you!) I continue to think that, in fact, *you* are the one who is helping *me* to mature and accompanying me on my path.

3rd reaction: And Marc? For now he's keeping his heart strong because that is what is needed, but we must also take care of him.

4th reaction: *Petons* and *una abraçada*

Magda / March 10, 2014

Thanks for answering my WhatsApp with such good humor.

During all this time, I have learned that this disease affects not only me, but the whole extended family I am fortunate to have, and my friends and colleagues who are also very supportive. I think sending the news with a bit of humor makes everything easier to bear and the people around me suffer less. For example, tone of voice is important when you talk on the phone, especially with Anna, my parents, my mother-in-law, etc. They draw a lot of information from this small detail, and you can calm them a lot with just a little effort.

I think there is also a "genetic" trait in this way of being. My maternal grandfather, whom I never met because he was killed during the *[Spanish]* Civil War, always said there was no need to worry until your neck was a meter away from your body! And my mother has transmitted to us this calm and confident view of life. The Heras genetics are absolutely the opposite . . . everything is dramatic and they often worry about things that never even happen.

I must say that doing the survey about the wig is fun. Most men like redheads and the "girls" something more "normal," but my mother said it wouldn't be bad to make a radical change and become a redhead, like an older woman in her neighborhood who uses a wheelchair! I think it's great Mom has that "attitude" at age 84!

I wanted to talk about something I have been turning over in my head for some days. Coming with Marc to visit you is very good for both of us, but it leaves me less time to comment on something that interests me. I will explain it to you here, and if you want to talk in person maybe I could come up one day or else by email, which is always more convenient but perhaps more aseptic.

Regarding the final outcome of my illness, I have thought for a long time now that nothing will happen to me that God does not want. This thought, which I must have "inhaled with the Psalms," has helped me a lot when they are doing the imaging (a bad time because they always find something new), or during a hospital stay. When I'm fine, I never think about it! When I pray the Lord's Prayer and say "Your will be done" . . . there are moments that something rebels inside me and I feel like saying, "and especially let it coincide with mine, which is to heal me!" Therefore, I have this bit of intellectual "schizophrenia" that confuses me. However, I believe that this thought helps me to go get test results and discuss treatment options with the oncologist without making a big deal out of it. For example, today when she told me I did not have the mutation for which there is an experimental drug in Vall d'Hebron, I thought: "Well, maybe it wouldn't have been right for me. It is still an experimental drug that has barely been tested. They will give me the chemo that seems to have worked."

On the other hand, Marc took it worse, maybe because he thought the experimental drug was my solution! As you said so well in your WhatsApp, Marc looks after me very well but is very worried and I have no other way of easing his suffering than encouraging him to continue doing his work and conference activities as normally as possible. In fact, he was about to cancel the Dubai course but I think it was a sign of normality that he went there. Besides, I have the luxury of having sisters, a brother, nieces, and nephews who show up without being asked.

Anyway, that's my reflection on "the divine will" . . . By the way, the parsley is flourishing out on the patio and every time I see it I think, "darnitall! I hope 'HE' is pulling that out of His ears once and for all."

I'll end with that little irreverence, and I am confident that tomorrow the chemo will go well. In the morning I also have a wig fitting, and I hope to "score" with the style.

You don't know what joy it gives me to know that you are on the other side of the email and that you will think of something to tell me that I can use when I am the most "down."

Have you heard anything from the *Escolania*? Have they landed in NY? I sent a WhatsApp to Sergi this morning, but he hasn't answered me.

Thank you for everything. If with this chemo I feel better, maybe you could come down one afternoon and have supper with us. Of course, it's Lent and I don't know what your limitations are. You decide for yourself; you are invited any time you want to/can come.

Ignasi / March 10, 2014

Thanks for your email, Magda. It is precious, in the sense of being "very valuable." We'll talk about it.

On Tuesday the 25th, I have an appointment in Terrassa with the ophthalmologist, and since they always dilate my pupils I would be very happy to have your company. We'll work out the details.

Sergi has written saying that they arrived well. They send news via the *Escolania* Twitter feed (but sending smoke signals used to be so lovely!).

Magda / March 11, 2014

You can count on me on the 25th. Tell me the time, and if you will stay for supper. That would be great, because Marc usually arrives at eight in the evening and so we could share some time with him, who also needs it.

This morning I'll visit the hairdresser (wigs) and at 5:00, the new chemotherapy. I'm looking forward to it, because I have to get better, and at the same time I am afraid of "the unknown." I will explain as I go along if you still have patience!

Magda / April 10, 2014

I'm not going to Madrid because of aphthosis in my mouth and oropharynx. Since yesterday I've been on a cold-liquids diet (ice cream, fruit smoothies, flans . . .), the dream of any child; but it has me in pain, and sometimes "crabby" (you'll forgive me) because I had worked hard on the symposium tomorrow and I cannot be there.

What a Lenten season Somebody has prepared for me! . . . We'll see if I notice any change with Easter.

Maybe I'll come to Vespers if I'm in a better mood. I don't like to complain, but I wanted to share this with you.

Ignasi / April 10, 2014

Mcgmbhgfdfvczsbdfrrrrrrr !!! and patience . . . If I could take on some of the aphthae for you, I would do it gladly.

Magda / April 10, 2014

Now we can see you on the Internet, so I will be at Vespers virtually; and don't worry, I can take care of the aphthosis myself (for now).

Magda / April 13, 2014

Una abraçada from Isil

We're having very beautiful spring weather, and now there are cherry blossoms and trees are beginning to green, but there's still a lot of snow in the mountains. All in all, a sensational landscape that I would like to enjoy for many years yet!

I wanted to ask for a favor: Can you tell me the schedule of the Easter celebrations? (i.e., those that you will put online.)

Today when I put on the Conventual Mass you were already reading the Passion. I looked at the calendar that is posted and it says nothing about the schedule, except that today the Conventual started at 10:30.

The aphthosis keeps getting better, and today was the first day I could eat lunch without lidocaine and could have solid foods.

April 17, 2014

Dear friends and family:

It's been awhile since I've shown any signs of life in the form of these little updates, but I'm still here! The last time I also wrote from Isil and that alone tells you this is a place where I try to spend time and where I'm inspired to be in touch with you.

The months of November, December, and mid-January I felt very good. I went back to swimming and the gym, so I asked for (and got) permission to return to work. I was back at the hospital only three days, the week before being readmitted to the hospital; it confirmed for me that I love my job. Unfortunately, I'm back on medical leave, and probably for a long time.

Most of you already know that I was admitted in February due to recurrent fever and was given a two-week course of powerful antibiotics to finish off whatever bug I had—and they almost finished me off too, because in the end the diagnosis was "fever of unknown origin" (a typical favorite on the list of options!). Since I was already at the hospital, they did the PET scan ahead of schedule and found a progression of the hepatic disease they had suspected from the most recent analyses. After a liver biopsy, they decided to change my treatment.

I have had two courses of the new treatment, one intravenous and the other oral. If, as the oncologist says, the efficacy is directly proportional to the side effects, I must be "cured." This time, my skin and mucous membranes are reacting as if it were their "spring," bursting out all over—and besides, now I'm a member of the "Red Band Society" *[Polsercs vermelles, a drama series on Catalan TV that inspired a short-lived American series of the same name]*, without a hair of stupidity *["ni un pel de tonta," a Catalan expression for "no dummy" and Magda's way of saying she has lost her hair]*. I already have a great wig and various scarves for variety. I look a little different, but I'm sure you'll recognize me.

Despite these inconveniences, every day I feel better in terms of capacity and desire to do things. Isil is ideal to test my physical stamina, as the weather is splendid these days and invites walks to various places. The landscape is spectacular, because the spring is just beginning—the cherry trees are blooming, we still see a lot of snow in the mountains, and the trees are just starting to leaf out. It's a fabulous spectacle that I love watching, and sharing with Marc, who takes care of me and pampers me and is always at my side when I'm "in a bad mood," which does happen because, as you can imagine, not everything is "flowers and violins" *[meaning something like "peachy keen"]*.

As I continue to enjoy your affection and companionship, you really don't know just how much it helps me. This is truly an experience that must be lived to understand it. In the meantime, I continue accumulating the "wisdom" this stage of life has to offer me.

Una abraçada and a Happy Easter!

Magda

Magda / April 17, 2014

I have finished the Gospel of Saint Luke. I do not remember ever having heard chapter 20, verses 27-39, and also haven't managed to clarify what it means (We married people have it worse?).

While I ponder these things and before beginning Saint John's gospel, I send you this photo where you will recognize Saint John's Church.

Spring in Isil (Sant Joan)

Ignasi / April 17, 2014

The image is beautiful. My mother is here at Montserrat and I am going to have coffee with her. As for Luke 20:27-39, we will talk about it.

Magda / April 20, 2014

Happy Easter! I sent you a video of Bonabé with the Noguera Pallaresa,[5] which is flowing mightily.

Magda / April 23, 2014

Happy Feast Day of Saint George![23] It's a bit late but I wanted to wait for medical news today. I've been at the hospital since 8:00 this morning but it was worth it. Hepatic enzymes are normalizing and I no longer have hepatomegaly, and since Easter I have, frankly, been feeling better, after the Holy Week I had with the edema and my face infected with erythema.

As we talked about, that day at our house, maybe someone IS listening to me from above and "secretly" removes the parsley from His ears. A phrase I heard my mother say a few times just came into my head; it's from one of the Castilian mystics: "God writes straight with crooked lines" (Saint Teresa?).

I had a lot of "down" moments when it was hard for me to swallow anything or I could not stand the burning heat on my face, and again I thought that I didn't know if all this suffering was worth it. A woman of little faith? But the psalmists also have these doubts and that makes me feel better.

After the good news, I felt like when you're pregnant and you give birth and you think you don't ever want to go through that again, but you forget everything when you see the baby.

By the way, I did my homework and I have read all four gospels. The differences between them are very interesting. We have to find a moment to talk about it.

I am very happy because tomorrow I go to Madrid for a meeting of the Executive Committee of the Society *[Spanish Society of Cardiology, which publishes the journal Magda edited]* and in the afternoon to Seville for a congress where I will moderate a panel on clinical cases. After missing the last two, I am more excited than ever because I will see colleagues from the Mayo Clinic and others with whom I have maintained a great friendship.

Marc will accompany me, which gives me a great feeling of security. We return Saturday evening, too late for the eve of the Feast Day for Our Lady of Montserrat. I thought I'd like to come to the Conventual the next day, but I imagine that you must have so many commitments that it makes me a little nervous about asking you; however, given our mutual trust I think I can raise the possibility.

Well, a long email but now you have my checkup results, more personalized.

Magda the moderator

Ignasi / April 23, 2014

Your email has given me great joy. First for the good news and then because I see that the daily relationship with the psalmists has given you a deep spiritual experience.

On Sunday the 27th it's no problem for you to come up, if you want. You just need to confirm your car's license plate number. The cardinal from Barcelona usually presides over the Conventual Mass, but this year he will be in Rome for the canonization of the two popes (John XXIII and John Paul II); Father Abbot will preside and even if there is a bishop or two, it's much simpler.

You really made me envy your trip to Seville. I've been there a few times, and it's a city that I really like. And right now it must be "splendid."

We will get together for the conversation about the four gospels. I believe that the differences between them are proof of their authenticity and their historicity. To check this, you can do a very simple test: ask four different people to explain in writing the same occurrence; no two are ever the same.

Fr. Hilari went to the Generalitat yesterday to receive the Cross of Saint George, and tomorrow he is signed up for the community's excursion (we will be out all day—by the way, early in the morning (08:00) we will be in the Visigoth churches of Terrassa to pray Lauds). And he says that he feels well. *Laus Deo [Praise be to God].*

Magda / May 1, 2014

It was a pity that I could not come on Sunday, but I had a pre-syncope when I got up and it was not prudent to abandon my "supine" position on the couch. I saw the ceremony on the Internet.

I'm back in Isil, with Anna and Xavi *[her partner]*; Marc is in England "preaching" the latest news about his beloved carpals[24] at the annual meeting of the British *[Hand]* Society. I chose Isil, without hesitation, and he tells me that it hasn't stopped raining there, so I made a good decision. He will return Friday afternoon and will come up then.

After the third batch of chemo (Saint George's Day[23]), I went to Madrid and Seville where I moderated a panel of clinical cases. I had a great time, but I have to admit that on Saturday the 26th when I got home I was very tired . . . but I recovered.

It's too bad that I'm so weak these days, but I was given erythropoietin (for mild anemia) and I've had an unpleasant reaction; I hope to improve over the weekend.

I have already been granted absolute disability (in record time), and we are now looking at how I can combine being a pensioner with "intellectual activity other than previous work." I no longer have a position at the hospital, but this situation can be reviewed in August and after 30 months. One of the changes I had wanted to avoid but it was not possible. Now I hope that one day I can reverse it!

On Monday I have CAT/PET scans after the third dose of chemo; we'll see what news that will bring.

Here the galloping spring continues, with many more tender green leaves on the trees; it's cool with cloudy/clear patches, typical of the season. Very nice.

I hope you're well and we can see you soon.

Ignasi / May 2, 2014

Good morning, Marta:

Thank you for your email. Yesterday afternoon I went to La Seu d'Urgell to ordain a priest (a clear example of globalization: a guy from Sri Lanka, ordained in the cathedral of La Seu, with part of his family there— the ladies with beautiful dresses, really colorful, and many priests from the bishopric of Urgell, the Sri Lankan consul, people from the Aran Valley where he is working as an ordained vicar, and the bishop speaking in Catalan, Aranese, Tamil, Spanish, and English). Bearing in mind that for three days I have been "dragging around" a respiratory virus that has me "*destemplado*," as they say in Spanish *[out of sync]*, I feel as if I am floating on a large boat in the middle of the sea.

I hope the CAT/PET scans will show good results, and meanwhile enjoy Isil and the family as much as you can. How beautiful it must be!

Yesterday, both on the way up and on the return trip from La Seu (I did it all by car, in the afternoon), I very much enjoyed the landscape, so green and still snowy in the mountains, singing psalms and praising God for the wonders of creation (wonders that include the human person).

Ignasi / May 2, 2014

Sorry, Magda: I now realize that in the heading of the previous post I put "Marta." It must be the virus . . . or I'm already "losing it."[25] Another *abraçada*, which includes Marc, Anna, and Xavi (the one I know the least).

Magda / May 2, 2014

Here it is raining a lot, so it must be Marc that is bringing us the English rain. He arrives in Barcelona in an hour and then he'll drive up.

What an interesting story, that ordination of the priest from Sri Lanka. It's like history in reverse . . . before we exported and now we import!

I'm not surprised you sang psalms; you know them from memory. This is a beautiful time that wins your heart. The naïve question is: How do the plants know that they need to grow now and how do they do it all at the same time?

Of the days that work for you, I prefer the 9th, 12th, or 13th, and I don't care if it's morning or afternoon. If you want me to talk with Sergi, I can come when it also works well for him. I hope that by then you'll be over your cold and I won't catch it from you!

When I saw that you called me Marta, I thought that you were confused with the other women in the passion story! As often as you've read it recently, that would be easy.

I hope you get "cured" quickly from the cold that has been bothering you; if you treat it, it lasts for a week and if not, it lasts for seven days! The feeling of flotation that you describe is very well known to me, and very personal, especially with this chemotherapy + erythropoietin.

May 8, 2014

Excerpt from a letter Magda wrote to a long-time friend

Dear Jaume:

During these almost 20 months of illness, I have learned to enjoy things that I overlooked before, as this time of year was always crazy with extra work on weekends. I say this because I'm experiencing the beauty of spring. I remember being thrilled by it last year, but this year even more so. Now that I have time to myself, I can stop, look, and listen as everything is reborn—including my desire for my "intruder" to finally go away! I want to stay here, surrounded by nature, friends, and family. I pray always for more springtimes . . .

As I write this, I'm looking out at the rosebushes with their beautiful blooms that have just opened and at a fragrant yellow bouquet of broombush on the table and all the green in the background . . . I hope to see you soon, with time to talk about everything.

These days I'm fuming because I have been put on "total disability" and that means I cannot officially practice medicine. I feel orphaned. I hope that, when this decision can be revisited, the "diagnosis" can be changed. What a dirty rotten trick, not being able to work when I love my work so much! This is one of the things I'm handling the worst . . . but know I have to toss it in the bag with everything else and keep going.

Magda / May 12, 2014

Thank you as always for your time and your comments. I still have a few things in the inkwell that I wanted to ask you, but we will have time to do it either by email or on the 28th.

1. The comment of Saint Luke about those who dedicate their lives to prayer in comparison to those who find a partner. I do not remember chapter or verse but I sent it to you more than a month ago and you said that we would talk about it.

2. In Psalm 62, there is a contradiction that attracted my attention. He says: ". . . power belongs to God, and steadfast love belongs to you, O Lord." Why does the psalmist differentiate like that if he is actually talking about the same "entity"?

3. A curiosity. I noticed that after the short reading at Vespers, you do not say "The Word of God" as you do at Mass. Why is it different?

As I have commented before, in my "previous" life I would never have paid attention to these details but now I have more time and perhaps, as you say, am more hyperattentive.

Magda / May 14, 2014

Good news. I just left the doctor's office. Tests came out very well: a significant reduction in gGT and alkaline phosphatase. Normal transaminases.

The PET report was not done yet because only the most senior radiologist does them, and he's away for a few days. However, it is very likely that it will turn out much better, given the clinicals and the test results. New protocol this afternoon. Let's celebrate that!

Magda / May 19, 2014

I have not been able to connect to Vespers today. Are you having problems again?

I think I have already come through the "worst" of the chemo: a weekend of couch time, once around the yard, and more couch!

Ignasi / June 3, 2014

I am looking for the verse in the Gospel according to Saint Luke that you asked about, and I cannot find it.

Since early this morning there has been some problem with a water leak in the bathroom ceiling; a while ago there was quite a lot of water dripping. The "maintenance crew" doesn't arrive until after 9:00.

At 11:15 I have my last classes in Barcelona to finish the Liturgical Year course (actually, *Año Litúrgico [because it was taught in Spanish]*). I have had a good time teaching the class, but had the feeling that I was leaving many things in the inkwell.

I should still shave before leaving.

Although I have been thinking about it, I do not come up with a clear explanation of why in the Liturgy of the Word we say "Word of God" at the end of each reading during the Mass, and in the Liturgy of the Hours (Lauds, Vespers, Matins) we do not say it. And I think: "Magda must think: how can Ignasi not know this?"

About Psalm 62, I suppose it is a problem of translation to Catalan; I do not know what the original Hebrew says. I have a French translation done by a Jew, which is very literal and allows you to get an idea of what the original says. It goes like this: *Un, Dieu parle; deux, ceci, je l'entens: oui, l'énergie est à Dieu. A toi, JHWH, le chérissement; oui, tu payes l'homme selon son fait.* That is, "One, God speaks; two, I hear: yes, the energy is from God. Of you, JHWH, I beseech; yes, you repay a man according to his deeds." *[For the sake of argument and consistency in citation, the New International Version translation is the following: "One thing God has spoken, two things I have heard: 'Power belongs to you, God, and with you, Lord, is unfailing love'; and, 'You reward everyone according to what they have done.' " (Ps 62:11-12).]*

Anyway, Magda, you see that I'm still far from having the "multi-tasking brain" that I need.

I will continue looking for the reference from Saint Luke and solving the other forty things.

It makes me a little embarrassed to write these things to you, precisely you, who knows how to do so many things at once and you are having to face very serious ones. But I trust you enough to do it.

P.S. The other day with your mother brought up many emotions. . . . Listening to her was truly a gift from our Lord.

Magda / June 4, 2014

Thanks, Ignasi, for your email. I read it yesterday at the airport, returning from Madrid again (meeting with the associate editors and secretaries). I'm always very happy to hear from you.

From what you explained, yesterday was a complicated morning; I think that when there are things we take for granted and they go wrong, all plans are off and they leave us "out of order." I remember when I had the sores on my head (January 2013) and we ran out of natural gas; I had to wash my head morning and evening and we had no hot water!!!! How did you even remember about me with all the "chaos" you had going on? . . . but at least you don't have to put on a wig every morning like I do. It adds about 10 minutes to the whole morning "*toilette*"!

When you talk about my "multi-tasking" ability, I think it's a skill I've cultivated for many years and that has allowed me to "not miss the train," neither for my family nor for the profession, although I may have missed others . . . Per my conversations with you, I think you should also invoke the "grace" that helps in especially difficult moments. . . who knows?!, but in any case I like to think about it like that (that's why I am your student).

Have you thought about which days you will come to Isil? Marc will take three weeks of vacation, and it would be great if all three of us coincide. Waiting for your news.

Today, lab results pending this morning, and tomorrow, another onco visit and fifth round of chemo. I will need to re-fill my sack of patience to withstand the side effects. You will help me.

Magda / June 12, 2014

To control symptoms I took SERC, and it has given me many side effects, especially nausea and vomiting. Now I've stopped it but I still feel as if I were riding a horse on a merry-go-round.

Today I read an article in the *Ara* newspaper that made me think of the "feminist" conversations I may have dragged you into against your will. The title is: "Do we women renounce power?" by Giménez-Salinas. I agree 100%!

How are you and "my patients"? I still don't know which days you will come to Isil, but (egotist that I am) I would like to share a few days with Marc and you.

Ignasi / June 14, 2014

How are you? I hope you have been able to get down off the "horsies" and feel steadier now.

I have not read the Giménez-Salinas article yet; I hope I can do it in the next few days.

Last Saturday Father Abbot announced some changes in responsibilities at the monastery. Because the current head of the sanctuary is going to work in Rome, in our "general curia," Fr. Joan Maria (until now in nursing) will replace him and Fr. Emili Solano (whom you do not know) will become a nurse. Because for him everything is new, both Joan Maria and this servant here will try to help him as much as we can. So it is up to me to do "overtime" in nursing (to support nursing, to be more accurate). I do it with pleasure.

By the way, talking about vacations, I still—that's why I'm a disaster—do not have my vacation days set. Anyway, seeing how things are going, I think that I will be able to have some days in the second fortnight of July (not counting July 31, which is my saint's day and I have to be in the monastery).

I suppose you have already experienced that, due to technical problems, we cannot send the liturgical offices to MTTV for broadcast (TV by IP, they call it). It looks like the "TriCaster" (what names!) needs repair, which is the computer that makes it possible. They have installed a provisional one, but they explained I-don't-know-what about passwords they had forgotten, and the point is that TV on the Internet does not work. On the other hand, tomorrow we will broadcast the Conventual Mass over the local TV network. Anyway, the goblins (or demons) of technology continue to play tricks, but they will not be able to make us retreat!

I look forward to seeing you and to *"due belle risate"* [*a couple of good laughs*], as our Italian friends say.

Magda / June 15, 2014

Thanks, Ignasi, for the news. Yesterday I told Marc that I hadn't heard anything from you for days and your ears were probably ringing.

I continue with a "rotational sensation" when I turn my head to the left; to the right it goes much better and is almost normal. In spite of everything, yesterday we went to Tarragona for the wedding of one of my residents, and we stayed for the appetizer, but after an eternal wait—we still hadn't had supper at 11:00—we left in order to rest, because although the atmosphere was pleasant, when you have vertigo you need peace and quiet.

Today we heard the Conventual on the radio and, obviously, you. You do *[the broadcast]* very well and the explanations of the music are great. Since you do not provide written explanations, Marc proposed that we come to Mass with headphones so we can hear what you say on the radio.

Magda, accustomed to the churches in the US, where the composer and musicians are always in the bulletin, insisted that Montserrat should do the same.

Today's feast day (Holy Trinity) is difficult for me; I always think that I do not understand the meaning of the Holy Spirit, although I remember you told me one day that it's like respiration, at a time when I was basically dyspneic *[short of breath]*.

I knew that the TriCaster was not working because I made a couple of failed attempts. When it's back again, you'll tell us! By the way, on June 29th, Sunday, it's my 61st birthday and we want to come to Mass. Will there be any Mass other than the Conventual, always so full, or is it better that we come at 11:00 and celebrate afterwards? Congratulations to

Fr. Joan Maria on the new job. I don't know the "job description," but it must be a promotion for him. If you give me his email, I'll write to him! Too bad, now that I had gotten to know him.

As for summer holidays, would you like to stay from July 14th to 19th? The week of the 20th to 27th my sister will come with a friend of hers. Otherwise it could be from the 27th to 30th, but that is only three days. The first three weeks of August we will be there alone. Let me know what you prefer. Wednesday we are going to Paris, if God wills and my vertigo is better. Marc has a conference and Anna and I are going as "luggage." When we get back, we will go straight up to Isil for the festival of Saint John. Again this year, Xavi and Marc will each bring down a *falla*.[26]

Magda / June 20, 2014

I attach a text that was forwarded to me and that I liked. We can talk about it if we see each other soon.

Ignasi / June 20, 2014

Thanks for the text. Yes, it's interesting. The author is a priest who has always worked in the world of science (a rare thing in both fields, both the priesthood and the sciences). Therefore, when he writes about scientific issues, he knows what he's talking about, and when he talks about theological issues as well.

It seems to me a starting point for reflection. I believe that the subject of original sin cannot be dispatched so easily. But, above all, I believe that the person of Jesus of Nazareth, the

Messiah, is essential for a Christian. The Christian faith does not focus so much on the "God" mentioned in the text as on Jesus Christ, recognized as the Son of God and revealing the Father and the Holy Spirit. On Jesus Christ who died and was resurrected.

Well, I don't want to start the conversation out of turn; but the text lends itself to it.

During one of Magda and Marc's last visits to Montserrat, I asked Magda if she wanted to receive the sacrament of the anointing of the sick. In this rite, in addition to anointing the sick person with an oil blessed by the bishop, the priests who are present put their hands on him or her and pray for that person. I told Magda that in this way, among other things, Fr. Hilari and Fr. Josep, whom she had helped so much, could express their immense gratitude by praying for her and laying their hands on her. She accepted it with pleasure and on the 28th of June, in the afternoon, I administered this sacrament in the presence of Marc and these two monks, her patients, along with Fr. Joan Maria. It was a very intimate and very emotional ceremony. Magda, with her simple innocence, had asked me if it were necessary "to make some special preparation for this sacrament. Needless to say, it's new to me." Obviously, I replied that she was "very well prepared."

Ignasi / July 2, 2014

Hello Magda. How was the PET scan? Are you better?

Marc (on behalf of Magda) / July 2, 2014

We have the result of the PET scan! All visceral tumor lesions are controlled. The metastasis in the head is also looking good. The problem is the side effects: constipation, profound tiredness, and nausea. She is so weak that she asked me to write to you because she cannot.

We hope that once the radiation is finished she will recover quickly, because she is really having a bad time of it.

Una abraçada

Marc (on behalf of Magda) / July 10, 2014

Hello Ignasi:

I'm writing to you with an update on how Magda is. The truth is that she is moving along, despite the mishaps we have had. As you know, the tumor has sprouted in the cerebellum and that gave her a lot of instability, dizziness, and vomiting. She was treated with radiation therapy for two weeks and seems to be responding, despite the great tiredness that it caused. Unfortunately, when we thought that everything was under control again, urinary disorders and major constipation appeared. To see what was happening, they did resonance imaging and found another metastasis in the terminal roots of the spinal cord. The day before yesterday the area was radiated. In doing so, they noticed that she had severe urine retention, which motivated them to implant a permanent catheter, and, to top it all off, she now cannot control her bowels and I have to change her all the time.

And so here we are: surrounded by catheters, diapers, resonance images, radiation therapies, and doctors with worried faces. But we continue to move forward, facing off against the tumor (with humor).

Thank you for the many evidences of support you all show us. They are very therapeutic.

Una abraçada

Magda / July 17, 2014

First of all, thank you very much for your visit. As you saw, I am very weak and I continue more or less the same. However, there is good news that we want you to know about: we will be grandparents! Anna is pregnant. We found out on the day after the Saturday we came to Montserrat, but they did not make it official until yesterday when we saw the ultrasound.

Mother Abbess is like boiled chard, with almost no energy to do anything at all. I hope to recuperate someday. Let's see if you can help me do that.

Una abraçada

Ignasi / July 18, 2014

Congratulations on the news that you will be grandparents! And thanks for letting me know. Yesterday I went with my mother for medical checkups. Whenever we see Antoni, your colleague who checks the pacemaker, we talk about you.

I fully understand the tribulations of the Mother Abbess. I don't think she's boiled, as you say, because last Saturday she received me with her usual irony* (so healthy and so oxygenating!). What's happening is that she is in the hands of doctors and that, sometimes, complicates life.

If you think I can do something more to help you, you know I'm here.

Una abraçada and greetings to Marc.

> *Magda was sitting on the couch, very weak, and when I entered, she said, half smiling: "You will forgive me if I don't get up, won't you?"

Marc / August 2, 2014

I am writing this from the emergency ward of the hospital in Terrassa. It's five in the morning, Saturday, August 2nd. Magda must have aspirated during one of the many times she vomited yesterday. Tonight she had a high fever, with chills, diarrhea, and even worse vomiting. They are working to stabilize her, and tomorrow we will decide what to do. I sense that the end is not far away. I'll let you know.

Ignasi / August 2, 2014

I'm in Aiguafreda with my mother. Yesterday I said Mass at a summer camp in a house near Brull managed by the nuns from Cottolengo. I will pray especially for Magda and for you.

My God, what suffering! *Una abraçada*

Marc / August 3, 2014

Magda had a good night. Unfortunately, it does not seem that she will regain consciousness like yesterday. She responds to external stimuli, but it is not voluntary. I fear that she is now in an irreversible state of coma . . . . But she is not suffering at all, which is what we wanted.

Ignasi / August 3, 2014

Thank you for the information. Yesterday I was happy to have been able to see her. We must have crossed paths in the elevators. *Una abraçada*

Psalm 23

¹ The LORD is my shepherd; I shall not want.
² He makes me lie down in green pastures.
He leads me beside still waters.
³ He restores my soul.
He leads me in paths of righteousness
   for his name's sake.

⁴ Even though I walk through the valley of the shadow
   of death,
   I will fear no evil,
for you are with me;
   your rod and your staff,
they comfort me.

⁵ You prepare a table before me
   in the presence of my enemies;
you anoint my head with oil;
   my cup overflows.
⁶ Surely goodness and mercy shall follow me
   all the days of my life,
and I shall dwell in the house of the LORD
   forever.

Epilogue

Just after six in the afternoon on Sunday, August 3, 2014, the hour of Vespers, "at the time of the lighting of the lamps," as the sun was setting behind the distinctive serrated outline of the watchtower that is Montserrat, Magda found the path leading to the other side of life. There she was awaited by many who had gone before . . .

Mariona, the infant sister she could embrace for the first time;
Ferran, the only son of dear friends, whose days here were ended in vibrant adolescence;
Enric, her brother-in-law, taken so suddenly from his wife and two young children;
and the Mother Abbess, of course.
Oh! And Saint Paul, quite contrite and eager to explain himself.

Montserrat seen from Sant Llorenç del Munt

Glossary of Terms

1 Conventual Mass (*missa conventualis*): This is the daily Mass of the monastic community, open to visitors, which together with the Liturgy of the Hours (the times specified for prayer in the Rule of Saint Benedict) completes the official public services in the Church.

2 Magda's **diagnosis** was primary pulmonary adenocarcinoma, a non-small cell lung cancer (NSCLC) that is more common in women than in men and more likely than other types of lung cancer to occur in younger people and nonsmokers. The text refers to cancer-related tests and other medical terminology, including tests such as gamma-glutamyl transferase (gGT), alkaline phosphatase, transaminases, hepatic enzymes), symptoms (hepatomegaly, edema, erythema), and imaging technologies, mainly positron emission tomography (PET) and computer-aided tomography (CAT) scans. In Magda's case, CAT scans assessed the location, shape, and dimensions of her tumor and PET scans showed growth and activity.

3 Gosh-darn / Omigosh / Darnitall: Magda and Ignasi use mild forms of "un-cuss words" allowed by good Catalan mothers, and I have translated them to phrases permitted by my own mother. The Catalan originals are more colorful than any cussing I was not allowed to do, but the parental interventions had the same effect: avoiding a violation of the Second Commandment.

4 *un petó/petons* (a kiss/kisses) and ***una abraçada*** (an embrace): As explained in the translator's note, this standard "sign-off" is not translated in order to preserve the sense of a friendly embrace and/or cheek kisses given in greeting throughout much of Europe. In Catalonia, this is typically a hug or touch on the arm and a perfunctory kiss on each cheek regardless of gender.

5 Isil (altitude: 1163m/3815ft) is one of four small villages in the municipality of Àneu Valley (**Valls d'Àneu**), located in the county of **Pallars Sobirà**. **València d'Àneu** is the administrative seat. **Isil** has fewer than sixty houses, distributed along both banks of the **Noguera Pallaresa** river, which divides to form a tiny island at the center of the village. The village hall, parish church, and rectory are on this "island." *Source:* http://www.vallsdaneu.org/list/14/pobles/18/isil/.

6 *Escolania* is a choir school first documented in 1307 (the founding year is uncertain; the monastery was established in 1025). The *Escolania* today consists of fifty boys from nine to fourteen years of age from all of Catalonia. The majority of the choristers start in primary school and finish as they begin secondary school, based on the development of the voice. Magda's brother, a cellist, teaches music classes there.

The *Escolania* is an integrated education and artistic learning center, recognized by the Department of Education of the Catalan government, the *Generalitat de Catalunya*. During the morning hours, the choristers receive general education in all subjects. The afternoon is dedicated to music theory classes, choir rehearsals, instrument lessons, orchestra, etc. For centuries, the choristers have sung daily at the Sanctuary of Montserrat. *Source:* http://www.escolania.cat/en/escolania/history/

Fr. Ignasi mentions the singing of the *Virolai*, composed in 1880 to honor the Madonna of Montserrat, called *la Moreneta* and *la rosa d'abril* (the Rose of April, the month of her feast day): https://www.youtube.com/watch?v=7-Fkh3mUqWY.

7 **Rule of Saint Benedict** (excerpts): Timothy Fry, ed., *The Rule of Benedict 1980* (Collegeville, MN: Liturgical Press, 1981). See also http://www.osb.org/our-roots/the-rule/.

8 *Catechism of the Catholic Church*: http://www.vatican.va/archive/ENG0015/_INDEX.HTM.

9 *Marató TV3:* This annual telethon, sponsored by Catalan public television (channel 3: TV3) and its operating foundation, raises funds for scientific research into diseases which are currently incurable. It also informs the Catalan public about these diseases and explains the need for research aimed at preventing and curing them. Every year *La Marató* attracts an audience of more than 3 million viewers, collects an average of 7 million euros (more than $8 million USD), and encompasses more than 2,000 entertainment and informational events throughout Catalonia. Participants include well-known individuals from the world of music, theatre, film, and sports, who donate their talents just as many others volunteer their time. *Source:* http://www.ccma.cat/tv3/marato/en/que-es-la-marato/

Magda referenced the *Marató TV3* performance of "You Raise Me Up," by Sergio Dalma and the *Escolania*: https://www.youtube.com/watch?v=kkeu28NbXn0.

10 The **Letter from Saint Athanasius to Marcellinus on the Interpretation of the Psalms** is the reference document when Ignasi talks about "making the words of the Psalms our own." *Source:* http://www.athanasius.com/psalms/aletterm.htm.

11 *Hilari Raguer:* lawyer, historian, and Benedictine monk living at Montserrat since 1954. He established a journal of

ecclesiastical history and has published studies of twentieth-century Catalan history. In 2014, he received the Catalan government's highest recognition for service to Catalunya, emphasizing his research on the short-lived Second Spanish Republic (1931–39, with a symbolic government-in-exile persisting in Mexico until a post-Franco Spanish Constitution was passed in 1972).

12 *Palau de la Música Catalana*: Built between 1905 and 1908 by the modernist architect Lluís Domènech i Montaner as a home for the *Orfeó Català*, the "Palace of Catalan Music" was financed by popular subscription. The building is an architectural jewel of Catalan Art Nouveau, the only concert venue in this style to be listed as a **UNESCO World Heritage Site** (December 4, 1997). The modernist building is designed around a central metal structure covered in glass, which exploits natural light to make Domènech i Montaner's masterpiece into "a magical music box of all the decorative arts: sculpture, mosaic, stained glass and ironwork." *Source and photos*: http://www.palaumusica.cat/en/the-art-nouveau-building_23602.

13 *Saint's days*, the feast day of the saint for which a child was named, are still celebrated extensively in Catalonia—and formerly, were more important than birthdays in many families. "Magda" is short for Maria Magdalena, the saint whose feast day is July 22nd. During some historical periods (such as the Franco era), newborns could *only* be given a name from a list of saints and holy places. For example, Montserrat was allowed in Catalonia, and a "Montse" can be congratulated on April 27th. On page 84, the correspondence notes some confusion about a Saint John in the readings; Ignasi explains it was John the Apostle (December 27th). [See glossary #26 for the festival held in Isil on the eve of June 24th, the feast day of John the Baptist.]

14 *Oxygen saturation* is the fraction of oxygen-saturated hemoglobin relative to total hemoglobin (unsaturated + saturated) in the blood. Normal arterial oxygen is approximately 75 to 100 millimeters of mercury (mm Hg), so 92 was an excellent saturation level. *Source:* https://www.mayoclinic.org.

15 *Crackòvia* (a take-off on Krakow, Poland, in Catalan) is a TV3 parody of sports news and figures, with a focus on Futbol Club Barcelona (*Barça*): https://www.youtube.com /watch?v=ZsGx3XF2FoY. In some parts of Spain, Catalans are the butt of "Polack jokes," but the jeering was turned into two highly popular and politically charged programs in news (*PØLØИIA*/Poland) and sports (*Crackòvia*/Krakow) commentary. (A "crack" is a spectacular expert or "pro" . . . like Barça's Lionel Messi, an Argentinian who has played his entire stellar career with the team.)

16 *La Mercè*, the feast day of Our Lady of Mercy, one of the patron saints of Barcelona, is also a major city festival: http:// lameva.barcelona.cat/merce/en.

17 *La Despensa del Palacio* (The Palace Pantry) is a famous pastry company that traces its origins to 1743 in Seville: http:// ladespensadepalacio.com/en/la-despensa/our-story-the-origin -of-a-name/. Note also that a muffin is called a "*magdalena*," and Magda's full name would be Maria Magdalena.

18 *Asterix and Obelix*: Comic books, originally in French, described by Ignasi and cited by Magda: https://www.asterix .com/.

19 *Referendum*: A referendum on seeking independence from Spain was a platform issue in the September 2012 parliamentary elections in Catalonia. On December 12, 2013 (a week before Magda's trip to Madrid), the new Catalan Parliament had voted to hold the proposed referendum and had set a November 2014 date. The central government in Madrid quickly declared such a referendum illegal. The political confrontation was in the news at the time (and persisted at the time of this translation, five years later).

20 The word *"pray"* is in quotation marks, in the translator's understanding, not because of any suggestion that the request is for "so-called prayer" (of course not), but rather because of emphasis or perhaps a double meaning of *"prega per mi"*: to send prayers and also to "ask" or plead (in this case, perhaps due to Magda's anxiety about the PET scan: Plead on my behalf).

Magda's request might suggest a play on words but the monk's response is unambiguous and heartfelt: Not "I will pray for you," but "I pray for you."

21 *Los Chiripitifláuticos* was a children's TV program in Spanish, characterized by slapstick humor: https://www.youtube .com/watch?v=yB_7g7_gsqk.

22 *La Moreneta*: The Virgin of Montserrat, one of 160 Black Madonnas documented worldwide (http://interfaithmary.net /locations/), is popularly called by this diminutive for "dark woman."

23 *Saint George (Sant Jordi)* is the patron saint of Catalonia, and this feast day (April 23rd) is also the International Day of the Book. As a minority culture that has fought hard to preserve its language and identity, Catalans celebrate the feast day of Sant Jordi with great passion: https://www.barcelona yellow.com/bcn-photos/113-pictures-la-diada-de-sant-jordi -barcelona.

24 *carpals*: Within Marc's expertise as a traumatologist and hand surgeon, his specialty is the carpal bones, best known as the "tunnel" that protects the nerve and tendon flexors that bend the thumb and fingers.

25 *losing it*: Ignasi uses the expression "making *catúfols*," the parts of a waterwheel that dip into the stream or river, rising full of water and returning empty. Making this piece did not require great precision or strength, so the task was usually given to older carpenters. The expression implies impending senility. *Sources:* https://unxicdellum.cat/2011/11 /fer-catufols/ and http://www.diccionari.cat/lexicx.jsp ?GECART=0028040.

26 *una falla*: A large, burning log carried on a runner's shoulder at a traditional festival for John the Baptist's Saint's Day held in Isil (and a few other towns). On June 23rd, the log carriers dash down the mountainside; the run takes about an hour and from the village plaza looks like a river of flame. At the bottom, the runners cross the river bridge and continue through the cemetery and village with the burning logs, then toss them into a huge bonfire in the plaza to celebrate the beginning of the feast day (Sant Joan, June 24th). A throwback to pagan celebration of the summer solstice, this tradition was dying out but was reactivated in 1978 and declared a festival of national interest by the Catalan government (*Generalitat de Catalunya*) in 1991. Photos are available at: http:// patrimonifestiu.cultura.gencat.cat/Festes-i-elements-festius -catalogats-o-declarats/Sant-Joan/La-Festa-de-les-Falles-d -Isil.

Afterword

Dr. Carlos Macaya
for the Executive Committee
of the *Sociedad Española de Cardiología*

The Executive Committee of the Spanish Society of Cardiology (Spanish acronym, *SEC*) unanimously approved a motion to fully endorse the publication and dissemination of this book, and gave me the privilege of preparing this brief message.

I met Magda Heras at the end of the 1980s, during her time at the Mayo Clinic in Rochester, Minnesota. When she returned to Hospital Clínic in Barcelona, we began an excellent professional and personal relationship, which included her inseparable spouse, Marc. During Magda's term as president of SEC's Ischemic Heart Disease Section, her well-established international reputation and personal relationships enabled her to bring prestigious cardiologists to enhance our section's annual meetings. Magda was proud of her work as a clinical cardiologist (and became the cardiology department head) and was also a rigorous and insatiable researcher. She began with the harsh, sometimes devastating, work of basic research but quickly translated her research findings to clinical practice: most of her publications were original research articles and at least 32 were multicenter studies. Her vocation for teaching was accompanied by excellent communication skills, and for this she was justly rewarded in 2006 by being made a professor at the University of Barcelona.

During my term as SEC president (2009–2011), I had the good fortune of being able to convince Magda to become editor-in-chief of the society's journal, *Revista Española de Cardiología* (REC), although I must admit that it was not easy to do. As the editor of REC Supplements, she was already very familiar with REC operations, but her reflective nature meant that she analyzed everything meticulously, especially the risks, before saying yes. I eventually managed to "sell" her on the ease of high-speed train travel between Barcelona and Madrid and agreed to increase the staffing for the editorial team in order to get her to accept the position. Her initiatives were inclusive; I remember well how she formed the Ibero-American Cardiovascular Journal Editors Network.

In our four years together at Executive Committee meetings, we all had total confidence in her to carry out this very great responsibility. Her leadership of the young group of co-editors, which she had free rein to select, was unquestioned, as they themselves recognized: Magda listened, analyzed, consulted, but did not hesitate to make decisions. The interpersonal and working environment that permeated the entire editorial group was enviable.

More than four years have passed since the death of our friend and colleague, Magda Heras, but she did not want to abandon us: she left an enormous scientific legacy of good management, of good practice, and the most appreciated but perhaps less known in the world of cardiology, her legacy of humanism. Magda had a fragile appearance that camouflaged her great strength, which she demonstrated again during her two years of suffering; she knew how to balance her professional work on the editorial team with the agonies of her disease, which punished her even more with repeated tests and aggressive treatments. The most amazing legacy of all is this book, a correspondence (transfigured by new communication technologies) that occurred between one doctor—a woman of faith and a patient who is reaching the end of her life—and another doctor, Father Ignasi Fossas, who had become a Benedictine monk and prior of Montserrat Abbey. The book (compiled by Magda's husband Marc and Father Ignasi after her death) is an exchange of thoughts, emotions, and questions without answers, in which we find more tears than smiles. We sense much, much sadness, something that very often makes us turn to spirituality. At the same time, Magda has left us the image of her climbing those peaks of the Pyrenees of Lleida that she loved so much.

Immense humanity emanates from Magda and Father Ignasi in this discovery of the prayers of the psalmists. From their dialogue, we can all gain a lesson in what is most needed in the society in which we are living: humanity.

Translator's Acknowledgments

I am thankful to all who reviewed drafts of the translation: my husband, Joan Roca, for attention to cultural details and our friend Diane Berge for pages of notes on the first version; later versions were read by my longtime friend Isabel Sehe, an experienced caregiver and master teacher; Jane Earley, PhD, dean emerita of the College of Arts and Humanities, Minnesota State University, Mankato; my favorite sculptor, Mary Ann Osborne, SSND, Our Lady of Good Counsel, Mankato; as well as two college friends from Gustavus Adolphus, Orrin Alt and Mary Raber, PhD. Before giving the manuscript to these readers, I asked for and received assistance from the Benedictine university/monastic community in central Minnesota, including our friend Molly Ewing, her colleague librarian David Wuolo, and Alex Blechle, the patient graduate assistant who helped me resolve a long list of queries (all at Saint John's University, Collegeville, Minnesota) and Renee Domeier, OSB, who graciously answered almost all the ones we missed and added many extra bits of helpful information during my visit to the Monastery of Saint Benedict, Saint Joseph, Minnesota. Molly and Sister Renee also contributed thoughtful and encouraging comments on the translated text. Finally, Marc Garcia-Elias, MD, PhD, and Ignasi Fossas, OSB, reviewed the translation and my added explanations.

The Executive Committee of the Spanish Society of Cardiology (Spanish acronym, *SEC*) has supported the English- and

Spanish-language translations of this book, and provided grant funding to Liturgical Press that was used to enhance the graphic design of this edition.

For all this generous assistance and support, I am most grateful.

Author and Translator Biographies

Mª Magdalena Heras i Fortuny was born in Terrassa, Catalonia (Spain), and never lived far from the city of her youth—except as a visiting cardiology researcher at Mayo Clinic in Rochester, Minnesota, and at Mount Sinai Medical Center in New York City—but she eagerly traveled the world, often with her husband and daughter.

Ignasi Fossas i Colet was born near Barcelona, where he received his medical degree. He is a Benedictine monk, holds a degree from the Pontifical Institute of Liturgy in Rome, and studied management at IESE School of Business (Barcelona campus). He has served as prior of the monastery at Montserrat since 2011.

Elaine M. Lilly, PhD, is a freelance academic editor. Her business, Writer's First Aid, provides prepublication support for scientific/medical researchers whose first language is not English (mainly Catalan or Spanish). Her deep love for Magda and her extended family, for Catalonia (her husband's homeland), and for the Catalan language led her to translate this book into English.